MANAGING THE BLUE LINE

POLICING THE POLICE

HOW TO IMPLEMENT, AUDIT, AND SUSTAIN EFFECTIVE POLICING STANDARDS

CHIEF CHET EPPERSON (RET.)

LITTLE CREEK PRESS
AND BOOK DESIGN
MINERAL POINT, WISCONSIN

Little Creek Press.
5341 Sunny Ridge Road
Mineral Point, WI 53565

ORDERING INFORMATION
Quantity sales. Special discounts are available on quantity purchases by corporations, associations, and others. For details, contact info@littlecreekpress.com

Orders by US trade bookstores and wholesalers.
Please contact Little Creek Press or Ingram for details.

Printed in the United States of America

Cataloging-in-Publication Data
Name: Epperson, Chet, author.
Title: Managing the Blue Line / Chet Epperson
Description: Mineral Point, WI: Little Creek Press, 2023.
Identifiers: LCCN: 2023907323 | ISBN: 978-1-955656-54-2
Subjects: LAW013000 LAW/ Civil Rights

Book design by Little Creek Press

Cover and interior photos: Shutterstock

This book is dedicated to the following—
my God who has guided, directed, and provided
my direction in life; my wife, children, and immediate family
for their support, encouragement, and love; to law enforcement
officers who go about everyday serving and protecting our country;
individuals in our country who now have an additional resource
to challenge and hold accountable the police.

TABLE OF CONTENTS

PREFACE

In 2014 I began to develop my thoughts on writing a book on my police career, specifically as police chief. At the time, policing had experienced high-profile events close to Rockford, Illinois, including the officer-involved death of Michael Brown in Ferguson, Missouri. I remember watching the Ferguson rioting and thinking how Rockford, Illinois, was so fortunate not to have experienced a similar response from the community after the in-custody death of Mark Anthony Barmore by police in Rockford. Ferguson and Rockford were similar cities in terms of police-community tensions and social, political, and educational challenges.

I am now satisfied that it took me years to complete this book as I grew from my retirement as police chief and distanced myself from the inner-police culture. Stepping away has allowed me a deeper appreciation of our department's successes during my tenure as police chief. Many people want change, but few want to change personally. Many people want to avoid controversy and would rather avoid such tough discussions. Many people would rather just get along and go along instead of challenging the status quo. Many don't have the inner strength to lead in a challenging environment.

Today, the policing profession is being challenged by many internal and external forces. Some of the challenges are the result of law enforcement not thinking strategically and getting ahead of the curve. Thus, chaos and confusion result in law enforcement agencies unable to withstand the tough and challenging conversations, meetings, and community unrest. Law enforcement can overcome their current complex issues with tough, bold, and courageous leaders who can manage the blue line amidst the storm. I hope you enjoy this book and are challenged by those who took a leap of faith to make the tough choices.

PURPOSE

This book discusses how to effectively manage the blue line as a police chief in an urban policing environment. Specifically, the book covers practical applications from actual encounters and experiences as an urban police chief. The purpose of such a book is to enable the reader to gain an understanding of how one maneuvers around challenging the status quo police environment to bring about effective police reform and efficiencies to those we serve. Many individuals, including the police, have limited exposure to the complexities of challenging the status quo. The policing industry is a tight and often resisting culture that does not like change or the process of change. Many police agencies retain police officers who are internally focused, myopic, and unable to see the trees in the forest. When an agency has a close-minded focus, it inhibits growth and the ability to see outside one's minimal look upon the larger issue of community connections and engagement.

This book is dedicated to allowing the reader to gain a wide perspective on challenging the status quo and assist other aspiring police chiefs in seeing firsthand the challenges they will encounter in managing the blue line. Some will review the book to learn the real and unedited version of an urban chief who challenged an organization. Serving as a police chief is a rewarding experience and a fantastic opportunity, especially in an urban environment when the social, political, and economic forces come at you full speed. You will have little time to dodge the competing interests as an urban police chief unless you have done your homework and staked your ethical ground. I dedicate this book to those who have provided me with direction in my preparation as a police chief and those who guided me along the way during the challenges of being that police chief.

As I ventured into the thought process of managing the blue line, limited resources were available to assist aspiring police chiefs who wanted to lead and manage the blue line. There are few reading guides on how to lead as a police chief. My main goal in writing this is to afford the rising police chief the opportunity to assess, appreciate, and ultimately learn some important components of managing the blue line in an urban setting. Also, this writing will allow the residents and interested parties to learn more about the inner workings of the police chief who manages, confronts, and challenges the status quo of American policing.

I encourage aspiring police professionals who wish to join the ranks of an urban police chief and those who can appreciate the complexities of a police chief and their role in urban responsibilities and input on *Managing the Blue Line*. You may think, "Urban street policing? What is this?" My definition of urban street policing is those law enforcement officers who work in a municipal city and contend with the complexities of poverty, lawlessness, community tensions, school educational deficiencies, unhealthy individuals, and a lack of financial resources to manage the day-to-day functions of government. These are just some examples of what local law enforcement officers experience daily when they police their cities.

This book will demonstrate and detail the inner workings of an urban police chief's perspective on crime, personnel management, economic realities, and making tough decisions. Many have encouraged me to write this book as there are few, if any, similar books available for the aspiring police chief. At the same time, I will offer the public—our community—the opportunity to see the challenges and difficulties of an urban police chief managing the blue line. I want to offer the realities to those young professionals who aspire to be the "chief" the opportunity to prepare now for the challenges they will encounter in the first few days of their role as an urban police chief. They will need to prepare hard to be the top cop and do their homework to survive and fulfill their role as the chief. I have purposely chosen to keep this book as positive as possible.

I am sure I have offended many in my professional and personal life, and I apologize. My intent in my personal and professional life has been to be the best and expect the best. To excel, one must be committed to the cause, have a mission, and then execute the mission. Keeping strong and focused on the mission alleviates the side steps and causes one to be off balance. Like you, I have encountered those who have purposely attempted to sidetrack my mission. Like then and now, I pray for those to recognize their shortcomings and inability to capture their own self-direction. I am a lifelong learner and believe in my profession, but I want to make it better and more accountable. This book will focus on the positives of managing the blue line.

You may ask what it means to manage the blue line. *Managing the Blue Line* will focus on policing issues woven around poverty, education, housing, economics, race, politics, and culture. Policing is called upon to solve some of today's most complicated social issues. Most of the time, police officers are unequipped, and the deck is stacked against them because of the deep-rooted issues of race and poverty. Being a police chief in an urban setting is even more difficult because the chief must manage and foster positive relationships within this complicated environment. *Managing the Blue Line* will provide the reader with an inside look at the challenges of today's policing environment.

I added discussion points at the end of each chapter so the reader can explore further their thought process about each chapter and its content. The chapters are short and provide the reader with the real-life experiences of an urban police chief. Our industry does not do a good job of creating a deeper involvement in important topics, which impacts our profession and sometimes disconnects with the community we serve. Hopefully, the continued discussion will provide thought-provoking discussions.

This book is dedicated to my wife and children. You offered your unwavering support over the years and provided the steadfast love and encouragement a man could only appreciate. I especially thank you for your patience, encouragement, and honor in serving our community with your family support. To my God, who afforded me the opportunity to be an urban police chief and provided the wisdom when to speak and the courage to stand tall when it was the right thing at the right time for the right reasons. My God supported me in the darkest moments and provided the shining light to do His will.

INTRODUCTION

I remember watching the 1991 Los Angeles Police Department Rodney King incident and the subsequent rioting. I happened to be in the Los Angeles area during the incident and attached to the television, observing a policing crisis. Being a six-year police officer on the streets of a large Midwest police department, the incident interested me. As a young police officer, how could I learn from this incident? Could I gain any takeaways from what was taking place in L.A. and incorporate lessons learned back into my work as a patrol officer? I watched the comments and strategic moves of the police chief, various police critics, comments of the mayor of Los Angeles, a retired LAPD captain, residents of Los Angeles, and the American Civil Liberties Union closely.

How could I gain perspective on this national policing issue? My first reaction was to the duration of the incident and the amount of force used by the Los Angeles police officers against Rodney King. Not only was the incident a humbling experience, but the following months and years were void of real discussions about what had occurred. Other than the Christopher Commission Report, which was well done, there were missed opportunities within our policing industry.

Our profession did not take the opportunity to determine what occurred, why it occurred, and how law enforcement could learn from the encounter. Fast forward fifteen years, and I found myself in the role of an urban police chief who had to contend with a persistent violent crime issue, strained police-community relations, a lack of a clear and articulate police mission, and an unclear vision for our officers to problem-solve in the field.

My mission and vision, as expressed to the Board of Fire and Police Commission as a police chief applicant: empower our officers, engage the community's residents, and instill accountability within the police organization. These concepts were long overdue and needed in our community. I was appointed police chief on April 10, 2006, and retired on November 13, 2015, after serving for over thirty-four years as a police officer. I served ten years as chief and was one of the few longest-serving police chiefs from a large Illinois city. My ten years were sometimes exciting, frustrating for short periods, and a lifetime dream fulfilled.

OFFICER-INVOLVED POLICE SHOOTING

I had been chief for about three years, and the department had begun several initiatives to reform the department. Specifically, the department started administratively investigating an officer-involved shooting incident. An administrative investigation is different from an Internal Affairs investigation. The administrative investigation reviews the incident from a policy, training, tactical, and equipment standpoint. An administrative investigation is not a formal or complaint investigation; it is administrative in nature and looks at the entire officer-involved shooting incident. An internal investigation is one where there is a specific complaint against an officer for alleged police misconduct.

On August 24, 2009, at about two in the afternoon, I received a call from a police commander who was on the scene of an officer-involved shooting (OIS) at a church—an incident that I consider an altering event for our city and the police department. Two police officers had chased a young male into a church, then into a daycare where several children had been present. The officers located the subject hiding in a utility closet and attempted to take the subject out of the closet when a fight ensued over the suspect grabbing one of the officer's firearms. The suspect was shot and killed in the daycare area. I arrived at the church, which was crowded with police officers, investigators, church personnel, and neighborhood residents. I was briefed on what took place. I examined the location of the shooting and observed the deceased male, who was still handcuffed. I could not understand why the deceased male had to be handcuffed, so I immediately instructed the handcuffs to be removed. I then spoke with the involved officers, who were shaken by the incident.

A large crowd had started to gather outside of the church. They were angry and yelling, growing increasingly louder. After experiencing several years of policing, I gained some understanding of angry crowds after a police incident. I proceeded toward the angry crowd and sensed their frustrations by their yelling and the looks on their faces.

I spoke with the individuals in the crowd, and the decedent's father was present. Some continued to yell while I attempted to address the crowd and told them what I knew. The crowd was not happy with what I told them. Many in the crowd were angered and spoke about their history with the police department. It appeared past police-resident interactions were not good, and I sensed much resentment and anger. The crowd did not hold back and expressed their frustrations with the police department.

I left the church and drove back to the police station to gain additional information. The shooting began in a church and ended in a shooting incident witnessed by young children. The days ahead were challenging for the two officers and their families, the decedent's family, the community, and other police officers who had to police the community.

So, have you imagined yourself in this shooting situation? Have you prepared yourself to address the national media? What will you say to national civil rights leaders such as Reverend Jesse Jackson and Louis Farrakhan? What will you say to your local NAACP director? How will you address your rank and file? They will want you to publicly back the officers, although you have not concluded the shooting investigation. The investigation continues with interviews and forensic evidence evaluation. How will you manage the day-to-day police operations and focus on this shooting incident? Many in the community will want "a minute" of your time to talk. Many will have opinions, suggestions, comments, and complaints, and some will curse your decisions. Some will go public with and attack your decisions, and some will never speak with you again because of the decisions you make.

When you raised your right hand and took your oath of office as the police chief, you took the oath to uphold the laws, regulations, and civility of your organization. You are expected to take charge and protect all individuals. Your oath of office does not cover the protection of special interest groups, clubs, organizations, retired and current police officers, and the "good ole boy" network. Your oath of office commands you to act with the utmost equal protection for all and maintain the civil rights of all. You are a servant leader and cannot serve more than one master. One that serves many masters will soon perish as the pressures and demands to please will outweigh the unwillingness to act strong under the pressures of many, and you will ultimately lose your focus and your vision.

THE NEXT DAY

The next day, I was requested by a local pastor to accompany him to the church where the OIS occurred and speak with some pastors. The pastor invited me to attend to converse with the pastor of the church where the shooting had occurred. There was to be another pastor in attendance. I arrived at the church and observed a local television crew filming in the parking lot. I called the pastor who invited me and told him I thought there would be no media. He got back to me and said the TV crew was filming outside, and he was sure they would leave soon. He told me to enter at the front of the church to avoid the television crew. I entered and was escorted to the pastor's conference room. The room was filled with more than thirty clergy members, and most of the clergy were from the city's African-American churches. Some men had collars around their necks, some wore suits, and some had full African wear with matching hats.

This was no informal meeting. These men wanted to talk, and I was their guest. I was asked to sit on one side of a long table, and all of the clergy sat on the other side. I was alone on the other side, except for a revolving fan that attempted to cool my side of the table. It was a hot and humid August day in 2009, especially inside the church conference room. I wasn't sure if the added temperature was due to the lack of ventilation in the room or the sense of anger from the men I was about to speak with. Prior to speaking with your local civic organizations or providing a TV interview, you would usually have time to prepare your thoughts. You would determine the latest crime stat numbers and update yourself on any tragic accidents and the latest community policing projects. This meeting did not allow me the opportunity to prepare. On this day, I did not know in advance who would be in attendance, and there was no agenda as to what they would like to discuss.

I walked into a room filled with men who wanted to talk, air frustrations, and hear from the chief of police about the shooting and overall policing relationships between the African American community and the Rockford Police Department. This was not the time to provide answers such as, "I will get back to you. I am not sure; let me check on those questions." No, the hour had arrived for answers on how I was going to lead the police department. Of great interest was the most recent shooting and long-fueled anger on how the police department interacted with the community and specifically the community of brown and Black.

Several questions were asked about the shooting, but I had limited answers because the incident had just occurred. I did have answers on what I would be doing with police-community relations. I heard the anger in most of the conversation. Some of the two and a half hours were spent by the African American ministers expressing to me their frustrations in past police-community relations incidents involving the police department. Most of the time, I listened to them speak about how the police treated individuals in our city in the past, how police shootings by the police were not properly investigated, and how police complaints were not properly investigated. These men were very upset. This meeting provided me with a historical perspective of how the police department engaged the community and especially its minority members.

At the conclusion of the meeting, the ministers told me they liked what I was doing as police chief and, similarly, the position of Mayor Morrissey, but they did not like the police department. What a statement! I knew then that I had much work to do. The meeting was not a report card on the recent police shooting but a look back into the agency's history and how our police-community relations were strained and needed repair.

I look back at that meeting and am so happy I attended. Prior to speaking before the ministers, I said a simple prayer to myself: "Lord, allow me to speak with the truth and protect me with what I say." There is no sense in going into every detail of what was said that day in the meeting. Those in the room know what was said. I heard the frustrations of the African American community loud and clear. The meeting made me a stronger individual and police chief. I learned about truth and reconciliation from those in the community who did not have a positive attitude or relationship with the police. Some of the ministers had firsthand experience with the police, and some were simply representing their congregations.

If you're ever invited to attend such a meeting in your tenure as chief of police—attend. Attend with an open mind. Attempt to hear what others are saying. I left the meeting after two and a half hours of listening and speaking very little.

The OIS involving Mark Anthony Barmore created much tension in the community between African Americans, police officers, and supporters of the police. Threats were made toward the involved officers, and their pictures were distributed throughout the city. Pro- and anti-police groups were planning marches. Several national civil rights speakers arrived in our city and demanded justice. After meeting with the local clergy, I pondered why there was so much tension between the police department and the community.

1970s INCIDENT

I searched online and discovered some public newspaper files of past police-community tensions. A similar incident from the late 1970s had similar findings to our most recent incident. An officer stopped a car for a traffic violation, the driver fled from the officer, and a foot pursuit ensued from the minor traffic violation. The driver fled into a church, and the officer subsequently arrested the driver for fleeing from the officer. The incident resulted in tension between the department, the African-American community, and religious leaders. I did not find any mention of all sides getting together and discussing the situation. None of the community leaders took the opportunity to discuss police actions, protocol, and what officers should do in these dynamic situations. In the end, there was much public bickering over the police incident. The incident made its way into the city council chambers during a weekly council meeting. A councilman and former police chief became entangled in an open and heated discussion over police-community relations and the incident. The mayor intervened and stopped the tense dialogue between the chief and the alderman.

I could not locate anything in the public files to indicate the police department or community ever coming together to discuss the incident. This was a good opportunity for the police department to reach out and learn from a segment of the community who did not have good feelings about the police department. It was also an opportunity for civic, religious, and civil rights groups to collaborate and bring their complaints to the police department. The department's actions could be reviewed to learn how future events could assist officers. I looked back at this incident and found missed opportunities for the police department, city officials, and religious and civic leaders. This was a perfect time to converse with those in the community who did not have good feelings about the police department. The community should have demanded conversations and dialogue with those who felt mistrust by the police department. The entire community missed an opportunity to come together and discuss what occurred, why it occurred, and how to move forward.

1980s INCIDENT

Tensions never seem to go away but remain in the minds of those who have issues with incidents. Fast forward to the mid-80s, and the police were informed about an individual who had not taken his medication for some time and was in the neighborhood being loud and out of control. A patrol officer located the individual, and the male ran from the officer. The officer pursued the subject on foot and finally caught up to the individual, who was rather large and tall. The male turned around and began physically struggling with the officer. The individual had the officer on the ground and was on top of him.

Another patrol officer came to the officer's assistance and tried to pry the male's arms off the officer's neck area. The individual was too strong and was not releasing his hands from the officer's neck area. The assisting officer took his long flashlight and struck the individual across the head. The strike caused the individual to release his hands from the officer. The two officers and assisting officers loaded the individual into a police van and, not knowing what to do with the individual, transported him to the police station. The officer who struck the subject across his head went into the police locker room and changed his pants as they had ripped during the struggle. Another officer watched the individual who was brought into the police station. The officer exited the locker room, and the individual was propped up alongside a vending machine. Finally, the officers decided to transport the subject to the hospital instead of taking him immediately after being struck in the head. The subject was pronounced dead at the hospital.

I can remember the evening and events, and at the time, the police station was open to the public twenty-four hours a day, seven days a week. An officer was stationed at the front desk. Individuals, including the media, could enter the building to file a police report and obtain information about crime and news stories. As this event unfolded, the department decided to lock down the police station. I have never heard of a lockdown of a police station unless there was some criminal act or threat of violence. No one, specifically the media, was allowed inside the police station. In this case and the days ahead, the department did a horrible job of public communication. As you can imagine, the next day's paper's main headline was about the police station lockdown. The lockdown took the front headlines and gave the appearance that the department was covering up the in-custody death incident.

There was picketing in front of police headquarters and comments from the NAACP. Again, the incident resulted in none of the parties discussing the actions of the police and the event that occurred prior to the in-custody death. Two of the officers were charged with several internal department violations. The Board of Fire and Police Commissioners conducted a hearing for the charged officers. The department officers were upset with the final decision, and for some time, there was a slowdown in police officer-initiated activity. The slowdown resulted from miscommunication from the administration regarding explaining what occurred the evening of the incident. Officers had to learn what happened through the lens of the media. Although the final actions of the board were correct, there was an opportunity for the department to have a fuller discussion about what occurred and how to prevent future tragedies.

From the late 1970s until 2009 is a long time for three police incidents to occur with no dialogue between the police and the community. The two prior incidents did not result in any after-action reports or policy revisions, new training, or tactical considerations. It was more or less business as usual—two incidents resulting in death and strained police-community relations. We expect our police officers to be the best trained and know how to de-escalate incidents when they can before a force incident.

ADMINISTRATIVE REVIEW

At the time of the Mark Anthony Barmore shooting incident, I worked with former Chief of Police Charles Gruber. Chief Gruber was introduced to me by Illinois State Police Lt. Colonel Rick Rokusek (Ret.) who was well aware of the issues I was dealing with internally with the department. Rick arranged a meeting for Chief Gruber and me to meet. We met in early 2007 and immediately clicked and developed a solid relationship. Our friendship continued through my tenure as police chief until his unexpected death in 2021. Chief Gruber mentored me on police organizational leadership and, specifically, the use of force. Before the Mark Anthony Barmore incident, Chief Gruber assisted our department in several portions of use-of-force organizational management. The Mark Anthony Barmore shooting incident stalled our forward trajectory.

Chief Gruber immediately suggested an outside independent administrative review of the shooting incident due to the complexity of the event and the public sentiment. Chief Gruber recommended Attorney's Christy Lopez and Kelli Evans, former United States Department of Justice civil rights attorneys now in private practice and monitoring a police department under a federal civil rights consent decree. The review was considered an after-action assessment of the shooting and, at the same time, an examination of the department's protocols and systems. The attorneys interviewed several police personnel, elected officials, residents in the community, and activists. The report and the findings were made public. The report's public release was transparent and open and served as a foundation for our department to improve. The city retained the two attorneys, and they began to review the shooting incident administratively. The retained attorneys were not investigating the shooting incident but rather assessing the incident from a policy, training, tactical, and training perspective.

COMMUNITY RELATIONS SERVICE

In the days after the shooting incident, community tensions grew fast with frustrations over the shooting of a male in a church daycare and in front of young children. Death threats were being made, community members were discussing rioting, and tensions were divided in the community over the shooting incident. Complaints were being made to congressional offices and the Department of Justice. A couple of days after the shooting, I received a call from the United States Department of Justice Community Relations Service (CRS). CRS works with community groups to resolve community conflicts and prevent and respond to alleged hate crimes arising from differences of race, color, national origin, gender, gender identity, sexual orientation, religion, or disability. First, CRS met and conferred with all stakeholders in the community—city government, police union, religious leaders, civil rights groups, community members, and the police department. CRS conducted listening sessions with each group to determine the tensions in the community and the recent shooting incident. All the groups gathered to discuss their differences and tensions and address the core issues. Additionally, the city had several anti- and pro-police demonstrations as a result of the shooting incident. CRS assisted by attending the marches to ensure everyone's rights were respected.

CRS then conducted a series of monthly meetings with all stakeholders, and there were several small group meetings outside of the monthly meetings. The meetings allowed everyone to voice their opinions and frustrations about the police shooting and the relationships with the police department. Many in the community and I spent a considerable amount of time every week in sessions to discuss police-community relations. The meetings were historical views. Some in the mediation sessions would address issues of police brutality from twenty years ago. Some would speak about police profiling, and some would talk about the lack of thorough police internal investigations. Many in my command staff and I spent over two years in the mediation process, and because of this, I believe our police agency was stronger and more disciplined when I retired in November 2015.

THE ADMINISTRATIVE INVESTIGATION REPORT

The administrative investigation report contained a holistic view of the August 24, 2009, police shooting incident. Prior to releasing the report, a meeting was held with the city council to discuss the report. Meetings were held with the command staff and supervisors, and the comprehensive, direct report was released to the public through a press conference. The report provided a self-critical analysis of what occurred and an assessment of the department's response and investigation of an officer-involved shooting incident.

I was very grateful to the city administration, specifically Mayor Morrissey, for providing the leadership in supporting the retention of such an endeavor. Looking back, very few police chiefs and mayors would seek out and retain experts to evaluate an officer-involved police shooting. Too many police chiefs do not have the courage to take risks for a self-critical analysis. It is very dangerous to seek such a review, as many police chiefs will fear the loss of support from their special interest groups and others that they are not supporting the police. What they are missing is the fact most police chiefs support their department and police officers, but few police chiefs are willing to take the risk and peek over the line and evaluate an officer-involved shooting. Chiefs fear what they will discover in the review process. Many are afraid of losing their job and status in the community. If a police chief requests an outside review, many, if not most, will require political backing from the city's chief executive. In my case, I was surrounded by many competent city administration personnel and especially Mayor Morrissey, who supported such outside reviews. In the end, the review would improve the department with enhanced policies, practices, and protocols.

The *Rockford Register Star* newspaper covered in detail the release of the Barmore Report and the recommendations.[1] The city conducted a public press conference and provided the *Rockford Register Star*

---

1 *Rockford Register Star*, June 16, 2010; June 17, 2010 articles.

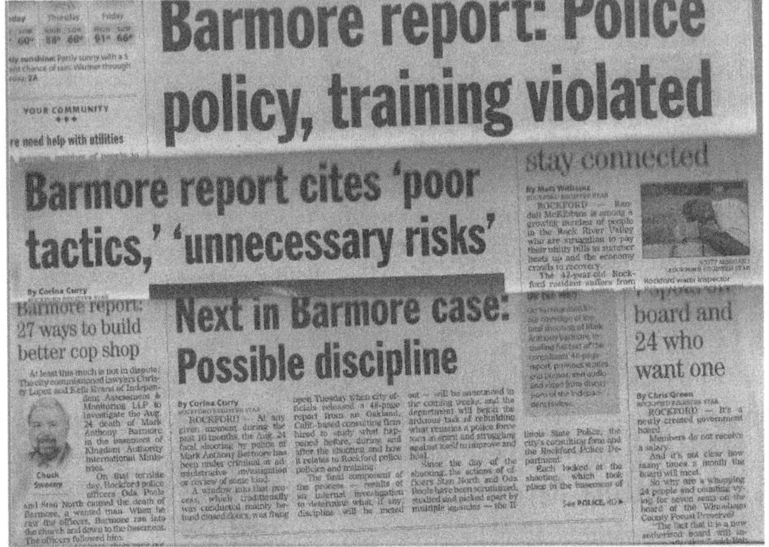

Barmore report: Police policy, training violated

Barmore report cites 'poor tactics,' 'unnecessary risks'

By Corina Curry

Barmore report: 27 ways to build better cop shop

At least this much is not in dispute: The city commissioned lawyers Christy Lopez and Kelli Evans of Independent Assessment & Monitoring LLP to investigate the Aug. 24 death of Mark Anthony Barmore in the basement of Kingdom Authority International Ministries.

Chuck Sweeny

On that terrible day, Rockford police officers Oda Poole and Stan North caused the death of Barmore, a wanted man. When he saw the officers, Barmore ran into the church and down to the basement. The officers followed him.

Next in Barmore case: Possible discipline

By Corina Curry

ROCKFORD — At any given moment during the past 10 months, the Aug. 24 fatal shooting by police of Mark Anthony Barmore has been under criminal or administrative investigation or review of some kind.

A window into that process, which traditionally was conducted mainly behind closed doors, was flung open Tuesday when city officials released a 48-page report from an Oakland, Calif.-based consulting firm hired to study what happened before, during and after the shooting and how it relates to Rockford police policies and training.

The final component of the process — results of an internal investigation to determine what, if any, discipline will be meted out — will be announced in the coming weeks, and the department will begin the arduous task of rebuilding what remains a police force torn in spirit and struggling against itself to improve and heal.

Since the day of the shooting, the actions of officers Stan North and Oda Poole have been scrutinized, studied and picked apart by multiple agencies — the Illinois State Police, the city's consulting firm and the Rockford Police Department.

Each looked at the shooting, which took place in the basement of

See POLICE, 4D

stay connected

board and 24 who want one

By Chris Green

ROCKFORD — It's a newly created government board.

Members do not receive a salary.

And it's not clear how many times a month the board will meet.

So why are a whopping 24 people and counting vying for seven seats on the board of the Winnebago County Forest Preserve?

editorial board with a briefing of the report before its release. Following are some of the newspaper headlines:

The administrative review report covered detailed information. The following were the major areas of the table of contents:

I. Introduction and Background

II. What Happened: What the Evidence Tells Us About the Shooting of Mark Anthony Barmore

III. Assessment of Compliance with Policy, Training, and Sound Tactics

A. Involved Officers Policy, Training, and Tactical Concerns

1. Entry into the Church
2. Attempt to Immediately Remove Barmore from the Boiler Room/Failure to Evacuate Children and Day Care Workers
3. Decision to Close the Distance on a Potentially Armed Suspect
4. Additional Tactical/Policy Concerns
   - *Lack of Intermediate Weapons*

- *Lack of Protective Vests*
- *Officer Supervision*

B. Non-Involved Officer Policy, Training, and Tactical Concerns

1. Misdirection of Officers by Dispatch
2. Lack of Active Supervisory Involvement
3. Immediate Investigatory Response to Shooting
    - *Officer Interviews*
    - *Video Recorded Walk-Throughs and Contemporaneous Officer Photographs*
    - *Recording Witness Interviews*
    - *Comprehensive Interviews by Designated Investigators*
    - *Use of Scene Diagrams and Photographs*
    - *Collection of Evidence*

IV. Assessment of RPD Systems Related to Prevention of a Response to Officer-Involved Shootings and Other Serious Uses of Force

A. RPD Policies and Practices for Reviewing Use of Deadly Force

1. Lack of Administrative Investigation of Officer-Involved Shootings
2. Ineffective Use-of-Force Review Board Process

B. Acceptance and Investigation of Complaints of Officer Misconduct

C. Early Warning System

V. Conclusion

The Administrative Investigation Report included twenty-seven recommendations as a result of the officer-involved shooting and an assessment of the department's investigations and risk management elements. After the report was made public, a steering committee was formed to ensure the recommendations were followed up and implemented. The twenty-seven recommendations were categorized into five task teams. The five task teams consisted of the following:

Task Team 1: Supervisory Responsibilities

Task Team 2: Administrative Investigations of Deadly Force Incidents

Task Team 3: Interviewing Techniques

Task Team 4: Use-of-Force Review Board

Task Team 5: Early Warning System Policy

The steering committee comprised representatives from the mayor's office, legal, human resources, and finance departments. A member from the police union, the newly created deputy position of Internal Affairs, and citizens were part of the group. The functions of the steering committee provided overall direction for the recommendation implementation. A leadership committee was formed, which consisted of point persons for each task team, a deputy chief of professional standards, and an outside police facilitator. The task teams were charged with reviewing current policies, research policies and practices of other police departments, reviewing related training, and providing recommendations for policy, practice, and training improvements. The task teams consisted of police personnel who volunteered for each group depending on their interest and expertise.

The task groups met frequently, and at the end of the process, twenty-five of the twenty-seven recommendations were implemented. Two of the recommendations could not be accomplished due to collective bargaining agreements. The recommendations were completed within eighteen months of the administrative report. The recommendations were implemented because the department would be in a much better position to ensure officers and their encounters with individuals were conducted safely and efficiently.

Likewise, suggestions on investigations were made, and as a result of the administrative review, the Countywide Independent Task Force was implemented to conduct officer-involved shooting investigations. As a result of the administrative review, the city purchased a training simulator for officer scenario-based training. The simulator allowed real-life officer encounters with individuals who may or may not experience a non-lethal or lethal force encounter.

The administrative review report was the beginning of making improvements with the department on the investigation of officer-involved shootings and other important risk-management issues. The administrative review process became the department standard in future officer-involved shooting investigations. The administrative review process was also utilized in serious incidents such as police pursuits involving injuries and other incidents involving training, tactical, and policy concerns. The administrative review was comprehensive and served the purpose of self-critical analysis of department operations.

The Mark Anthony Barmore Administrative Review Report contained the following recommendations:

SUMMARY OF RECOMMENDATIONS

1. We recommend that RPD address questions about the officers' entry into the church during the administrative interview of each officer. We recommend further that RPD review its protocols and training related to building entry to ensure that its training and protocols sufficiently teach officers how to gather information and coordinate their efforts in such situations to maximize safety and effectiveness.
2. We recommend that RPD investigate whether the involved officers

considered using their available intermediate weapons and, if they did consider these options, why they chose not to use them. We further recommend that RPD determine why officers were not carrying all the intermediate weapons in which they were trained and take appropriate corrective action.

3. We recommend that RPD policy be revised to require all officers to wear protective vests while on duty. We further recommend that RPD assess whether the involved officers in this incident had a protective vest readily available to them.

4. We recommend that RPD evaluate its supervisory system and ensure that each officer is assigned to and actually works with a single, clearly identified supervisor.

5. We recommend that RPD work with the Rockford Fire Department to evaluate the actions of the dispatcher during this incident and take the corrective action necessary to prevent similar confusion in the future.

6. We recommend that RPD evaluate the actions of supervisors who were responsible for the involved personnel and/or geographic area in this incident. We recommend also that the Department determine whether its policies regarding officer and incident supervision are adequate to ensure proper supervision of personnel in routine and significant events.

7. We recommend that RPD revise policy and practice to provide notification of and response by representatives of RPD's Homicide/Violent Crimes Unit (or other designated criminal investigative entity); Office of Professional Standards (or other designated administrative investigative entity); State's Attorney's Office; City Attorney's Office; and Training Unit, to every high-risk incident, including all officer-involved shootings.

8. We recommend that, absent extenuating circumstances, RPD

require that officers involved in a use of deadly force, such as an officer-involved shooting, be formally interviewed about the incident prior to going off-duty. These interviews should be audio and/or video recorded in their entirety with no off-tape pre-interviewing.

9. We recommend that RPD revise policy and practice to require video recording of all scene walk-throughs by involved personnel.

10. We recommend that RPD revise policy and practice to require, except where there are extenuating circumstances, photographs be taken of personnel involved in serious use-of-force incidents while the personnel are still on scene and reflecting their appearance at the end of the incident.

11. We recommend that RPD require video recording of all statements in officer-involved shooting investigations.

12. We recommend that, to the extent feasible, one investigator, or team of investigators, conduct all interviews in each case. Where this is not feasible, investigators should closely coordinate their interviews. We further recommend that RPD provide additional training to investigators and require them to ask follow-up questions to clarify discrepancies and ambiguities.

12. We recommend that investigators be required to routinely use and retain diagrams and photographs to assist involved personnel and witnesses in describing events and to document those descriptions.

13. We recommend that RPD revise policy and practice to require that holsters and other parts of the involved personnel's uniform with evidentiary value are collected before the involved personnel leaves the scene of the incident.

14. We recommend that RPD revise policy and practice to require the collection and review of involved personnel cell phone records covering the time period after the use of deadly force incident

before the involved personnel provide their descriptions of events to department investigators.

15. We recommend that RPD take particular care in officer-involved shootings and other high-risk incidents to ensure tight control of the scene to restrict the number of personnel allowed access in order to avoid disturbing evidence and to maintain the integrity of the scene.
16. We recommend that RPD revise its use of deadly force investigation policies and protocols to require a prompt, separate, parallel administrative investigation of each officer-involved shooting, and require the preparation of a report documenting the findings of that investigation.
17. We recommend that RPD revise policy and practice to consistently *require* the Board to determine in each case whether the use of force complied with RPD policies and training; whether proper tactics were used; whether the actions of non-involved personnel complied with policy; and whether the incident was properly supervised and investigated.
18. We recommend that RPD revise policy and practice to require that the Department's legal counsel and personnel from RPD's Office of Professional Standards and Training Unit be required participants in Use-of-Force Review Boards.
19. We recommend that RPD policy and practice require that the administrative investigation report of an officer-involved shooting or other serious use of force be promptly completed and that the Use-of-Force Review Board use the administrative investigation report as the primary basis for its analyses and findings.
20. We recommend that RPD limit the participation of involved officers and supervisors in Use-of-Force Review Board proceedings.

In particular, all involved officers and supervisors should be excluded from the Board's discussions and deliberations.

21. We recommend that RPD require that Use-of-Force Review Board members have the requisite training, experience, and temperament to conduct probing assessments. RPD should provide clear expectations to Board members about their responsibilities to identify and respond to policy deviations and training and tactical concerns and ensure that Board members fulfill those responsibilities.

22. We recommend that RPD revise policy and practice to require the Use-of-Force Review Board to provide an explanation of its findings and recommendations in each case. We further recommend that RPD revise policy and practice to require documentation both of the approval or rejection of Board recommendations and of the implementation/completion of Board recommendations. We also recommend that RPD use the information that comes out of the Boards to develop and provide additional scenario-based training to officers. The training should include emphasis on pre-force tactics and decision-making, communication skills, and de-escalation techniques.

23. We recommend that the Department regularly evaluate all of its trainers, particularly its use of force, search and seizure, and other critical trainers, to ensure that they have the skills and temperament necessary to provide training consistent with RPD's mission and values and remove any trainers who do not.

24. We recommend that RPD revise policy and practice to remove obstacles to filing complaints of police misconduct and ensure that all non-frivolous allegations of misconduct are appropriately investigated.

25. We recommend that RPD evaluate whether the delay in entering this officer-involved shooting into EWS was an anomaly and, if necessary, revise policy and practice to ensure that all officer-involved shootings and other uses of force are incorporated into EWS within a reasonably short time period of their occurrence.
26. We recommend that RPD revise policy and practice to ensure that all uses of force and all misconduct complaints, formal and informal, be included in EWS. We further recommend that RPD explore the feasibility of entering key historical data, such as officer-involved shootings, into the system in order to provide supervisors and managers ready access to more complete information regarding their personnel. We also recommend that RPD evaluate the internal benchmarks and thresholds it is using to determine whether officers who may be in need of intervention are being identified by the system, and that such interventions are occurring and being monitored for officer improvement.

Going forward, the department managed officer-involved shooting investigations in a new manner. We implemented a Winnebago County Integrity Task Force, which consisted of law enforcement officers from police agencies in other county police departments. There, teams formed within the task force. In the event of a Rockford officer-involved shooting, no Rockford or county officer would investigate the incident. Officers from other agencies would assist under the direction of the Illinois State Police and conduct the criminal investigation. Likewise, if the county experienced an officer-involved shooting, no Rockford officer would assist in the investigation. The format was set up in this manner to avoid involvement with two of the larger agencies in the county having similar officers who were with each other on a daily basis to conduct their officer-involved shooting investigation.

DISCUSSION POINTS

1. Does your agency have an inter-governmental agency agreement with other police agencies to conduct officer-involved shooting investigations?
2. Is there a policy to govern such an agreement?
3. How are officers trained to conduct the investigations?
4. Does your agency conduct parallel criminal and administrative investigations?
5. What is the current status of the police department's relationship with the minority community?
6. How often do you meet and discuss police-community relations?
7. How often do you meet and confer with the leadership of minority civil rights organizations?

TENACITY

Some will wonder, will I address the issues of controversy from my close to ten years as police chief? The answer is one that I have longed to answer finally. I thought if the book is about addressing the complexities, then yes, I will share my experiences and challenges with challenging the status quo.

Taking over an entrenched and somewhat inner-focused agency was sometimes difficult, but being an inside-outside officer, I associated with a select few over my years with the agency. I kept busy finishing my undergraduate and graduate degrees, providing little time for extracurricular activities. Sociological, political, and criminal justice theories were my interest as I set a goal to lead the police agency and attempt to change our ways and methods. Right away, I began to develop methods and practices to enhance our organization. Coming off of the heels as a deputy chief, I positioned the department to manage crime control effectively. Instead of a chief providing the media with no reasons for crime upsurges, I wanted the agency to develop metrics and analysis on crime issues. This was accomplished by implementing crime analysts within the department, who could crunch the data and provide real-time crime information to our officers and community about crime, hot spot policing information to line officers, who could better manage their patrol beats, and association data on suspects, locations, and victims of crime for investigators who could enhance their investigations and solve cases sooner.

CRIME REPORTING

We accomplished much by being the first Illinois police agency to transition from the legacy Uniform Crime Reporting to the National Incident-Based Police Reporting System (NIBRS). Instead of reporting eight crimes to the government, police agencies report fifty-two crimes. Reporting the additional crimes allows an agency to gain a wider perspective on how to manage the crime issue. NIBRS allows an agency to assess crime-offender relationships, which can help others in the criminal justice system to assist with crime incidents.

Many chiefs and elected officials are petrified about speaking publicly about crime data, let alone reporting additional crimes. I was often surprised when I heard a chief could not explain why certain crime data increased or decreased. I remember vividly a police chief making a statement to the media that he knew the crime year over year had increased, but he could not provide any reasons for the increase. The chief's comments were out of touch. He should have at least conducted an assessment regarding the increase.

DISCUSSION POINTS

1. How does your agency communicate crime data to the public?
2. Is your crime data available to the public via the police department's webpage?
3. Does your department utilize social media to inform the community of crime incidents?

SYSTEMS

The rollout and implementation of technology was a good portion of my career, not only as a deputy chief but throughout my tenure as police chief. The department was very fortunate to have dedicated technical staff and the ability to make huge technical improvements to the police department. The following are some of the major technical improvements implemented over the years. There were huge technical implementation projects, which projected the department forward in quickly transmitting data to respond rapidly to crime incidents and solve crimes.

The department lacked a sense of mission and how to go about attacking crime from a holistic approach. For several years, our department and similar agencies attacked a problem by throwing resources at the issue—more officers and overtime. I could not remember a time when an opportunity for overtime was ever void of some officer not taking an opportunity to make additional money. Personnel are an organization's most valuable asset; most officers will do what they are instructed to do. Unfortunately, many times officers worked overtime with little or no direction.

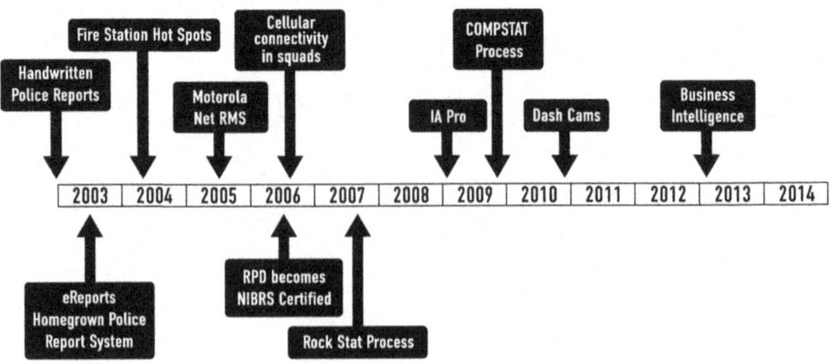

DISCUSSION POINTS

1. What technology systems does your agency have to communicate to the public?
2. What technology system does your agency have to maintain police accountability to the public?
3. How often does the police chief communicate serious crime issues to the public?
4. Does your police chief communicate the "police message" to the community, or does the head elected or appointed non-police government leader communicate the police message?

PROBLEM-SOLVING

An overlooked important area of law enforcement is how police agencies problem-solve. Some police departments use the concept of SARA:

S – scan the issue

A – analyze the scanned data

R – respond to the area with a plan

A – assess the results of what you did

This process takes some time but has a long-lasting effect on improving the quality of life and lessening repeat crimes. Our department began to use this method of problem-solving, which worked well in some of our most frequent areas of crime and overall quality of life issues. For example, if an agency receives numerous calls for service at an apartment building, a department first attempts to assess what is causing the repeat calls. This is the SCAN PHASE. In order to determine the overall picture of the calls, a management report is required in your computer-aided dispatch (CAD) and records management system (RMS).

In both of these standards, police systems will provide the following information: calls for a specific time of the day, number of responding officers, duration of the officers at the location, day of the week of the call response, arrests, if any, and other pertinent information. This is the ANALYZE PHASE. Data is collected, and the department will process the data and determine if there are any patterns, such as the time and day of the week for the repeat calls and type of calls.

In this example, an agency may discover that most calls require a fire truck, ambulance, and police officers. The reports indicate medical calls where someone needs assistance with their medicine, falls out of bed, or requires medical assistance and cannot live alone.

These data points are important and formulate the RESPONSE PHASE. The department will now convene with the building manager and other community medical resources to assist. For the next thirty days, the department will respond with an action plan and other community resources to assist with the repeat calls.

After thirty days, the department will enter the ASSESSMENT PHASE. The department will evaluate the results of the action plan. The department will assess and compare the calls for service from the past thirty days. If there was no decrease in calls for service, the department will re-evaluate its analysis and response phases and make any modifications. In most situations, if the data analysis and response phases are completed correctly, the department will observe a decrease in repeat calls for service.

I experienced tremendous value in the SARA method. It is easy to use and does not call on alone the easy answer—add more personnel and spend overtime. The SARA method is objective and attempts to get at the root cause of an issue. The SARA method can be used for many crime-related issues, including domestic violence, residential burglaries, speeding autos, shootings, and carjackings, to name a few.

DISCUSSION POINTS

1. What problem-solving method does your agency maintain?
2. Is the problem-solving method known to all members of the agency and community?
3. How does your agency communicate to the community its problem-solving strategies?
4. Does your agency publicly display crime data to the public?

WORKING WITH EX-OFFENDERS AND VIOLENT CRIME

One of the most overlooked aspects of municipal policing is the relationship between the police and ex-offenders. My definition of ex-offenders for this book is those who served time in a state or federal penitentiary. For several years, the police department had a festering problem with combating violent crime. For the most part, the department's crime focus was making arrests and working overtime to conduct the investigations. I took over as police chief in 2006 and immediately focused on creating an afternoon investigation presence. For the most part, the department maintained a Monday to Friday, eight to four investigation presence. After four in the afternoon, the department was void of any shift of investigators who could respond to violent crime incidents and conduct follow-up investigations. If a crime occurred after four, investigators would have to be called back and be on the clock with time and a half compensation. Why would anyone want an afternoon shift of investigators if you could void the afternoon shift, respond after hours, and make more money?

A more important area of concern is the demonizing of convicted felons. Over the years, I have witnessed law enforcement personnel who think, act, and treat convicted felons much differently from other individuals. I have had conversation after conversation with law enforcement personnel who are sure to tell everyone the person is an "ex-con." The label automatically stays with the person, and law enforcement treats the person differently, as if they are some foreign and strange element to be aware of. This horrible attitude leads law enforcement to view themselves as superior to convicted felons.

CEASE FIRE

One of the first areas of my involvement as police chief was the organization Cease Fire. "Cease Fire uses prevention, intervention, and community-mobilization strategies to reduce shootings and killings. The program was launched in Chicago in 1999 by the Chicago Project for Violence Prevention at the University of Illinois at Chicago School of Public Health. By 2004, 25 Cease Fire sites existed in Chicago and a few other Illinois cities. Some of the program's strategies were adapted from the public health field, which has had notable success in changing dangerous behaviors. For example, public health campaigns have helped to decrease smoking and increase childhood immunizations. In fact, the program's executive director, Gary Slutkin, is an epidemiologist who views shootings as a public health issue."[2] The Rockford Cease Fire Program was headed by Ralph Hawthorne, a committed individual who cared passionately and deeply for people.

The Rockford Cease Fire supported the police department by getting into troubled areas where police officers could or would not have ever been able to insert themselves. Cease Fire consisted of highly-trained intervention specialists who got into some of our city's most troubled crime areas and disrupted potential violence. Cease Fire also conducted marches and prayer services in those locations where there was a recent shooting or murder. Cease Fire struggled year after year with financial support, and the organization finally stopped due to a lack of funding. During my involvement with Cease Fire, I met the Reverend K. Edward Copeland, which was the start of great community engagement opportunities.

2 Nancy Ritter, "Cease Fire: A Public Health Approach to Reduce Shootings and Killings," *National Institute of Justice Journal*, October 28, 2009, https://nij.ojp.gov/topics/articles/ceasefire-public-health-approach-reduce-shootings-and-killings.

ALTERNATIVE DRUG PROGRAM (ADP)

I had the great opportunity to hear a presentation by David Kennedy at a Problem-Oriented Policing Conference in Madison, Wisconsin. A police commander had heard Kennedy a few years prior, and the commander wanted me to hear his presentation at the conference. The main theme of the presentation was that law enforcement had been arresting the same drug dealers year after year, and law enforcement was getting the same negative results in changing police-community relations behaviors. Kennedy had presented a new hope and practice of arresting drug dealers and making neighborhoods safe. That was when I had the opportunity to go public and gain the support of the local community clergy.

An immediate assessment was completed with the department's crime analyst. It was determined two geographic areas were contributing to the high percentage of violent crime, including drug selling. The data was displayed visually, and I conducted citywide meetings with governmental, business, religious, and educational leaders along with neighborhood groups. We needed assistance and partners from the religious community to assist us with the neighborhood chaos. I was summoned to meet with Bishop Washington, a long-time serving pastor in Rockford. Bishop Washington heard my presentation at one of the many meetings and believed there was something to the content. At the meeting, I again met with Reverend Copeland, who had frequented and supported Cease Fire operations. Bishop Washington blessed the program and had Reverend Copeland assist the police department in this endeavor. The Alternative Drug Program consisted of the following process:

First, we located any area in a specific community where the drug dealing was taking place (mapped the area) and conducted some surveillance to identify the drug dealer. The drug dealer was the focus, unless the buyer was armed with a gun or committed a violent criminal act during their drug purchase. Once the established dealer was located, an investigator would document the drug sales to individuals by day and time of the week. Surveillance photos and videos were then taken of the seller, along with securing as much personal information as possible, including place of residence, any employment, family status, and past criminal arrests and incidents. The drug investigator would then obtain a drug sale by either purchasing drugs from the seller or getting their informant to purchase the drug. Once the drug was purchased, the investigator would seize it and get it tested for confirmation of an illegal substance.

The investigator would then work up the case and determine the seller's current or past criminal record. If the seller was new to the criminal justice system, then the seller was eligible for the program. The program consists of the following:

- The seller is invited to a community forum. The seller is provided a formal letter from the chief of police and prosecutor of their recent selling of narcotics. The seller is told to show up for the meeting, and they will not be arrested but offered alternatives to their behaviors.
- The community gathers in a large area to discuss the drug selling in the neighborhood and calls to action to rid their neighborhoods of those drug dealers. The meeting lasts approximately one hour, with presentations by the mayor, prosecutor, local clergy, neighborhood leaders, and the police chief. The group applauds loudly and agrees the drug dealers must go.
- Prior to the end of the meeting, those who were personally invited (drug sellers) are now invited to come forward. The drug dealers are seated at reserved spots at a table with their name card. There is a three-ring binder with tabs in front of them. Every instance of them selling drugs is photographed for the drug dealer to see. Each tab has an unsigned complaint for every

criminal demeanor. A videotape is now shown for each drug dealer and their selling to the community. I can now see tears running down the eyes of most of those dealers present.

- The federal and state prosecutors now present how they could be arrested right now, but they are being provided a second chance. The second chance allows the dealer to make a decision: submit to a case management process or be arrested for drug dealing. The dealer would be permitted five days to make a decision.

For those who decided to seek assistance with case management met and were counseled for their social, emotional, educational, and financial well-being. Reverend Copeland was instrumental in coordinating the case management. For those who decided to seek case management, their drug dealing cases were dissolved after one year. There was a ceremony to honor those who went a year without drug selling, and their past criminal activity was eliminated.

The department conducted two drug market locations, and we referred to the locations as Alternative Drug Program One and Two. National criminologists' research was conducted for the two drug market areas, and it was statistically proven that both locations experienced a reduction in crime along with the entire city due to the process.

OFFENDER CALL-IN

Another community effort to hold returning offenders back from the Department of Corrections was the offender call-in. Again, Reverend Copeland was the community catalyst in this endeavor, along with our federal, state, and local law enforcement agencies and federal and state prosecutors. Mayor Morrissey greatly supported the program.

Offenders were invited to a monthly call-in where they were offered to either seek case management assistance or the "stick" warning that if they re-offended, they would be placed at the top of the list and prosecuted to the fullest extent. At the same time, the "carrot" was offered to each called-in offender in providing case management assistance for educational, housing, substance abuse, and counseling services. The program's duration was approximately two years, and after I retired, the process ceased at some point. The National Institute of Justice-Crime Solutions evaluated the process and offered some amazing results: The RAVEN intervention was associated with a relative reduction of 6.3 percent in total non-gun violence compared with the constructed synthetic control group. This difference was statistically significant.[3] The RAVEN intervention was associated with a relative reduction of 9.5 percent in total violence compared with the constructed synthetic control group. This difference was statistically significant.[4]

DISCUSSION POINTS

1. How does your police department engage with the community?
2. How does your police department engage with high-risk groups?
3. Does your police department share the successes of their community engagements with the community?
4. Are the successes measurable?

3 "Program Profile: Rockford (Ill.) Area Violence Elimination Network (RAVEN), National Institute of Justice, August 29, 2022, https://crimesolutions.ojp.gov/ratedprograms/766#

4 Ibid

POLICE PURSUITS

One of the most hotly debated issues a police chief will encounter is their policy decision on police pursuits. Most officers are eager to pursue a driver who takes off from them after the red lights and siren is activated. Unfortunately, many officers and I have witnessed the tragedy after a police pursuit. Today, there are many options other than pursuing an auto. Yes, there are times when officers should strongly consider pursuing a driver, but these incidents are rare. A more risk-managed approach is required to keep officers and the community safe.

After taking office as chief, I witnessed several incidents of officers involved in a police pursuit for minor traffic violations. Unfortunately, the policy permitted the pursuits. I immediately modified the policy in two ways.

First, the policy was modified with the following: “Using these criteria for initiating a pursuit, it is the policy of the Rockford Police Department that no pursuit will be initiated for a traffic offense stop. The pursuit will not be initiated, and follow-up investigation will be conducted for enforcement action.”[3][5] Thus, a traffic offense was not authorized for a police pursuit. Was there a no-chase policy? The quick answer is no. The department modified its police pursuit to prohibit the pursuit of a driver for only traffic violations, such as violating a stop sign, speeding, and taillight violations.

Second, an officer now had the opportunity to follow up on the traffic offender by completing a police report with information about the auto: license plate, make, model, color of auto, and a description of the driver. Officers then followed up on the auto in order to locate

5 Rockford Police Pursuit Policy, 2015

the auto, driver, and owner of the auto. Under the guidance of the city corporation counsel and city council, we developed an impound policy for such offenders. There was a tiered process for repeat offenders. This new process added value to our overall mission to keep individuals safe. We publicly reported the success of the process, and at one time, we had approximately sixty percent of those drivers who would not stop for police resulting in either the driver or owner being cited and the auto impounded. This process kept officers and others safe, while the department reduced its liability by eliminating police pursuits that may have ended in fatalities.

Another important component of police pursuits is the active role of the first-line supervisor, who is required to listen to the police radio, particularly when an officer requests to pursue a driver. The supervisor must be aware of the department's policy and quickly assess if there are enough reasons to allow the officer to pursue the driver and auto. Far too often, the first-line supervisor is not actively engaged in the direct supervision of a police pursuit. The lack of active management often results in bad outcomes. This is why the first-line supervisor monitors their officers and quickly determines if the pursuit aligns with department policy.

DISCUSSION POINTS

1. Does your agency have a limited police pursuit policy?
2. Are your officers required to seek supervisory approval before they initiate a pursuit?
3. Does your agency have an administrative review system to evaluate police pursuits for agency compliance, training, and equipment considerations?

LAW ENFORCEMENT INTEREST

My interest in law enforcement began at about the age of fourteen. My mother introduced me to a classmate from her grade school years at Sunday mass. My mom's school classmate was a police investigator. I was very impressed with my mom's grade school classmate, and my interest in knowing everything about the police department grew. The investigator was friendly and encouraged me to join the Rockford Police Department as a police cadet. The investigator was down-to-earth, straightforward, and very positive about the department and his profession. My mother's friend said I had to be at least eighteen to join the cadet program, and then when I turned twenty-one, I could join the department. I was excited about the opportunity. The cadet program was a feeder program to attract young members from the community and allow police cadets exposure to various functions of the police agency. As a young adult, I was fascinated by the opportunity to join the department right out of high school.

Three years later, I vividly remember taking the entrance exam for the cadet program. It was the same test for a police officer. The location was a high school gym on a Saturday morning. Over five hundred police applicants showed up, including several potential police cadets. I was impressed with the number of individuals in the gym, but it was also an intimidating process. The cadets completed the same entrance exam as police officers. What an experience to be in the same room taking the same test with individuals who wanted to be police officers, even though I would eventually be a police cadet.

I waited four years, and finally, the time had come. I was eighteen and started as a police cadet with the Rockford Police Department. On Monday, January 6, 1981, I was sworn in by the chief, along with several other police cadets and police officers. I remember the night before, when I was sworn in as a police cadet, I had become sick with nervousness about the opportunity. The cadet program was a great opportunity to learn about policing, working along with crime scene investigations, attending autopsies, learning the mechanics of photography, shooting a firearm, issuing parking tickets, learning about crime patterns and analysis, working with investigators on youth sexual abuse investigations, learning the fundamentals of fingerprints, and riding along with police officers. This was all one could imagine doing as a young person. I look back now over my forty years of policing and look at how the cadet program was the beginning of what I am today.

The experiences afforded me the opportunity to learn much from many and to avoid the areas of policing I did not like, such as the rough talk and coarse attitude of how some police officers acted, poor communication skills with complainants, lack of thorough investigations, and avoidance of spending quality time developing leads with criminal investigations. The cadet program was the beginning of my professional police career, which ended as the city's police chief. It was a decision I have never regretted. I often hear of individuals who regret their career choices, and to this day, I have never regretted my career choice and time as a professional police officer. My time as a sworn officer was the best career choice one could make as a young person right out of high school.

At the same time that I desired to be a police officer, I also wanted to obtain a college degree. I knew a college degree would enhance my skills and prepare me to advance in my professional career. It took me fourteen years going part-time as a college student and working full-time, but I accomplished my long-term goals of obtaining my BS and MBA degrees. Both degrees opened my horizons, professionally and personally. My degrees afforded me an excellent liberal arts degree in sociology, anthropology, and public policy.

In retrospect, the police investigator I met at church should have been the department recruiter. He was experienced, knowledgeable, and presented himself well for the department. The investigator was very encouraging and knew how to converse with a fourteen-year-old. Louie Palmeri, I dedicate a portion of this book to you and my mother, Beverly, who took the time to converse with someone inspired by your willingness to share your career conversation with me.

I thank my mother for her introduction to the police investigator and his positive attitude toward his profession. My mother often runs into Louie, and they have conversations about the police department. I am not naïve and still remain an idealist that adults do and can positively influence the youth of our times to provide good conversations and directions for one's profession. Thank God we still have positive influences in this complicated world.

DISCUSSION POINTS

1. Do you have a planned police open house on an annual basis?
2. Do you have a police ride-along program that encourages individuals to see firsthand the internal operations of your police department?
3. How do you use social media to convey your agency? Are the posts just about community engagement, or do you also post crime incidents?
4. What type of "feeder" process does your agency maintain to attract potential police officers?

PREPARATION

One of the first things an aspiring police officer should do if they desire to be the chief is do their homework. I have seen too many times an aspiring police officer who wants to be the chief, and the person conducts little or no due diligence. I have also witnessed police chiefs making foolish mistakes because they failed to see the big picture in their community. Once you become the chief of police, you still have homework to do. You will need to know the agency's financial and personnel management issues. Don't rely on someone to tell you the answers; you must do your homework. You need to "feel" the agency before you decide to lead. Can you imagine knowing nothing about someone before making a life commitment to them? It's a good idea to determine the city's revenue, expenditure trends, and overtime history over the past five years. What is the city's wealth, and how does Moody's rate the city's bonding ability? Is the city dependent on grants from the federal government at a rate that will hurt the city if the grants are taken away? How many employees would lose their positions if the grants were removed? One of the areas to check prior to signing the dotted line is the personnel management issues: discipline, sick time, training, and personnel policies. These four areas are critical components of an effective police agency. You must have all four running at the highest cylinders.

Lastly, what does the community say about the police department? Does the police department allow the community to voice their concerns to government leaders? Does the city provide community surveys on how well the department serves the residents? What are the relations between the citizens and police officers? Do residents feel safe and secure to make complaints against the department and officers? Does the city have a residency requirement for employees, specifically police officers, to reside in their city? If so, what percentage of police live outside the city? Why is there a residency requirement?

Find out what caused the residency change, and you may discover some deep-rooted community issues.

DISCUSSION POINTS

1. Review and assess the agency's organizational chart.
2. Assess the agency's budget and, most of all, the overtime budget. This is where you will most likely find issues. Most chiefs will not address and challenge the department's overtime dollars. Police officers depend on overtime dollars.
3. Review the department's disciplinary history.
4. Review the department's early warning system (more in later chapters).
5. What is the city's crime rate, and how is the agency addressing the high numbers?

ACCOUNTABILITY

Accountability is an often tangled and foreign word in policing. For some, the word accountability means to ensure coming to work every day, putting in eight hours, and receiving a paycheck for the work you provide. In the private sector, this is a common and known phenomenon. However, in policing, accountability is an overused word. Many police chiefs talk about accountability, but few rarely carry out the intent. Police accountability comes down to holding your organization accountable for public actions, practices, and customs. At times, it comes down to shining the light on an organization's internal processes and practices: ensuring the established protocols are meeting the organization's objectives, and supervisors and those in oversight positions are carrying out their roles; confirming these individuals are providing effective coaching, mentoring, and corrective action when necessary; and guaranteeing residents and visitors of a community are receiving professional policing services. Seems easy? These practices might be straightforward for some police agencies but difficult for many police departments and, more importantly, for police chiefs to manage.

Have you thought about how you will manage the blue line as a police chief? Are you contemplating leading your police agency in the future? Have you assessed your agency and city culture? In other words, are you ready and able to possess the elected political support and make reform efforts in the police department, which will most likely go against the grain of your agency? You will often hear many in the police profession state how on average, two to five percent of the agency personnel are malcontents and troublemakers. Agency leaders will often state we know who the bad apples are when a crisis occurs within the agency and involves one of the bad apples. Rarely do we hear law enforcement leaders addressing how their agency is ensuring they are "managing" bad apples and repeated police misconduct by a few in the organization. I observed, assessed, and made calculations on several elected officials and police chiefs before I was appointed chief of police. I listened, observed, examined, and witnessed good and bad leadership skills. My reviews were assessed at the local, state, and federal governments. Strong elected officials allow their police chiefs to carry out the police function collaboratively. The method begins with an accountable police chief who will hold themselves accountable for their actions.

Self-reflection and personal accountability are a must in order to hold others accountable. At the same time, elected officials and, more importantly, the chief-elected officer must have the full support and trust of their police chief. The chief-elected officer must allow their trusted chief to command control of the department without interfering with petty issues. The chief-elected officer must step aside and allow their police chief to address the community when it comes to crime issues. The chief-elected officer can and should support their police chief during a crisis, but the day-to-day operations and crime reporting should be left to the duties of the police chief.

DISCUSSION POINTS

1. How do you define accountability?
2. What systems will you set up as police chief in your organization to assess accountability?
3. How will you know if you are achieving your desired results?
4. Are you open and willing to publicly report your accountability assessments to the public?

5. Define your agency's accountability process. Most police agencies will state publicly and in writing that they have an accountable police agency, but few will be able to provide documentation of their accountability process.

6. Actions are more powerful than words, but specific objectives, which describe the agency's accountability systems, are essential to communicate with the public.

7. A police agency should provide the public with data metrics on the inner workings of their agency. The following are such examples:

   - Traffic stop data, broken down by area of city stop conducted, gender, race, age, reason for the stop, and outcome of the stop.
   - Pedestrian and field stops of individuals, broken down by area of city stop conducted, gender, race, age, reason for the stop, and outcome of the stop.
   - Resident-generated complaints against police officers. The complaint metrics should include the date of the complaint, the completed date of the investigation, the outcome of the complaint, and a listing of any officer discipline.

FIRST FEW DAYS

I remember the first few days as police chief. There were several murders in the first ten days of my new position as chief. I felt the criminal element initially challenged my appointment as chief. I put in long days and attended many neighborhood meetings along with various civic group gatherings. My message was simple: improve the quality of life for Rockford. The police alone would not solve the crime problem, but the key to success was mobilizing our community groups and neighborhoods. Arresting and re-arresting individuals would not bring about social change. Change would come with a comprehensive and solidified working relationship with what I call the three-legged stool: police, prosecutor, and judges.

These statements offended some because they felt they were being called out. Our police department sat too long and idle on an important issue of crime control. For the first time in my recollection, a police chief publicly spoke and said he needed the cooperation of the prosecuting attorney and judges to combat the crime issue. For far too long, the community had operated with just the police doing the heavy lifting, and when the crime went up, the police were called up front and center to explain why the crime was high. An arrest of an individual is the first part of the criminal justice system; the two other key components are the prosecution and disposition of the case. A comprehensive urban criminal justice system is one in which the crime, prosecution, and judicial sentencing rates are publicly discussed and made transparent for the community. Anything less is a lack of community transparency. Anything less does not address the root causes.

I had no personal agenda against the prosecutor or judges, and many have been good professional associates over the years. Unfortunately, there needed to be a closer working relationship and shared responsibilities with the crime issues. At times, I felt the crime issue was simply a police issue, and other criminal justice partners were silent on the issue. For example, the county spent millions of dollars purchasing a court case management system. The system's selling point was to have data metrics from the initial police officer booking of an arrested individual to the final court disposition. This seemed like a good and robust data system. After a few years of dealing with shootings and gun violence, during our open city accountability session called Rockstat, the mayor requested information on gun arrests, repeat offenders, and their court case disposition. This seemed like an easy task to obtain information from the county management system. Our records manager inquired about gaining the data. Instead of obtaining the requested data, we received a rejection and were asked if we did receive the information, what were we going to do with the data? It seemed like an odd response for requesting public data information. After some time, the data was finally released.

At times, I felt the request of information and materials from other governmental entities was an intrusion. I soon discovered government was not accustomed to providing data metrics about their work. There was an unwillingness to inform the public about local government performance. I was glad to work for a mayor committed to transparency, openness, and accountability. This paradigm worked well when we developed the COMPSTAT and problem-solving process while inviting the public to our public-open meetings.

The data, or Gun Stat as we called it, provided useful information on the offender's journey through the court system. The metrics demonstrated those who had previous court arrests, convictions, and sentencing outcomes for the gun arrest. Lastly, the data provided the names of those judges for their disposition of individual arrests. The information allowed an agency to assess gun arrests and the court process to determine if there were any evidentiary issues from the arrest or investigation. At the same time, the data provided a broad and wholesome picture of how the criminal justice system managed gun arrests. Time ran with my career, and I retired just as we were getting into developing a more comprehensive approach to the issue of gun crimes in our community. I don't believe that today the department uses the gun metrics to assess the arrest, prosecution, and judicial decisions on violent crime incidents involving guns.

DISCUSSION POINTS

1. What are the current impediments in your police agency?
2. What is the relationship between the police department, district attorney, and judges?
3. Are you able to measure the data metrics of your police department, district attorney prosecution decisions, and judicial outcomes?
4. What is the perception of the community toward the police and the entire criminal justice system?

CIVILIAN REVIEW BOARD AND COMPLAINT PROCESS

An area that continually presents mistrust between communities and the police is the use of members in a community to review police misconduct. For many years, police agencies have solely received the initial complaint of alleged misconduct, investigated the incident, and made the final determination of the incident in terms of any remedial action. The investigation and corrective actions are two areas of concern with communities. Some communities feel the police have isolated themselves, and at the same time, they do not provide a comprehensive investigation. Some community members feel police department internal investigators are simply associated with the very police they investigate. How can the police police themselves?

Unfortunately, many communities have had strained relationships over the years, and one particular incident can spark unrest between the police and the people. An incident will cause tension in a community, and a police chief must be prepared to handle the situation. Most of the time, a police chief will run for cover in an attempt to make things easy during a crisis. Unfortunately, this is too late, and a police chief must get ahead of the issue before it becomes a crisis and attempt to build relations. If a police chief tries to develop relations after a crisis, the result will likely not fare well for the chief. The attempts to build a relationship between certain community segments and the chief will be perceived as ingenuous at most.

Prior to being appointed as police chief, I decided if given the opportunity as chief, I would immediately lay the groundwork to mend prior strained relations within our minority community. After my appointment, I immediately attended nonstop community meetings throughout the city, gathered at houses of worship, began an open and transparent relationship with the media, and fostered an open-door policy for the community. For several years, there were too many missed opportunities, and the department fell short of mending relationships with the community.

After being appointed chief, I initiated a police chief's advisory board. The board comprised several members from the community: political, legal, community activists, labor, retired police commanders, youth, and concerned citizens. The board allowed me to hear the community's concerns and feelings about the police. Similarly, this was an opportunity for me to share the organization's successes, direction, and overall efforts with the community. We met quarterly or sooner if there was a significant issue within the organization. The board rotated semi-annually with new members, and at the end of my tenure, approximately twenty-five volunteer individuals participated with the board. This opportunity gained the community's trust and allowed the board to provide input, comments, and suggestions.

During an officer-involved shooting incident, several community members who lacked trust in the department vocally opposed the department and said it was not open and transparent. I remember one minister stated, with all due respect, "We were all cut from the same cloth." Although I was the chief, I was still part of the blue line and did not hold police officers accountable. Specifically, this group of community members did not believe the police department held an internal investigation fairly and impartially. I could not convince the members that the department had turned the corner and we were doing the right thing. My words were not enough to convince this group of community dissenters.

Therefore, I met and conferred with the union and gained their support in allowing the dissenters to come down to the police department and review some approved citizen complaint investigations. Internal

Affairs took three approved citizen complaint investigations and let the community members review the investigative files. We redacted the personal information from the files and allowed the members to review the complaint investigations. The members were able to review the initial complaint, interviews of witnesses, officers, attachments in the file and the entire Internal Affairs investigative file. Needless to say, the community members had changed their feelings about the complaint investigation. The community members were impressed by how Internal Affairs investigated all leads and information within the complaint. The community members were overly satisfied and convinced the department was acting professionally in handling complaint investigations.

This is an example of how police departments can gain the trust and respect of police departments. Allowing community residents to review case investigative files is an attempt for community members to learn firsthand about the complaint process. In the end, police departments will continue to struggle with citizen mistrust of police interactions. A well-trained citizen can and should be allowed into the decision-making process of their police department. Just like we train citizens on how to be police officers, departments can train, educate, and foster non-police officers to be part of the complaint process. Departments that allow residents to be part of the process will soon see how they can transform their agency into being open and transparent with the affairs of a public entity. The public is part of a police department, and every effort should be made to include in some capacity community members in the process.

During the same time of mistrust with the community, the local NAACP chapter president stated they had experienced individuals in the community who were uncomfortable coming down to the police department location and filing complaints against an officer. The individuals felt the police building was intimidating. I agree with the NAACP. You had to go through three layers of security before meeting with Internal Affairs. At the request of the chapter president, we implemented a complaint portal, which would receive an intake of citizen complaints. The portal at the NAACP office worked well, and community members were much more comfortable proceeding to the NAACP office rather than the police station to file a complaint. Over time, we realized these complaints of alleged police conduct would not have been received if the portal was not implemented. Community members would not have been comfortable filing a complaint at the police station where they accused an officer of misconduct. This was a fine example of effective community relations and bridging the gap between the police and particular community organizations, which had been broken over the years.

During my tenure, I was regularly invited to the Illinois NAACP State Convention to address police-community relations, specifically the use of force. The sessions were a great opportunity to connect with statewide community members who supported the police but had, at times, a mistrust of the police due to a lack of communication. In fact, I presented in a neighboring city, where the police chief did not attend the meeting. The chief did not send a representative, and the session was rather intense. At the time, there were several national police-involved deaths, and this particular convention had several concerns and questions.

Unfortunately, my experiences of citizen involvement with the complaint process are not shared by other police agencies. The police must find ways and methods to bridge the gap of mistrust between the police and the people. A cookie-cutter approach will not work, as one size does not fit all. Now is the time for enhanced citizen involvement in the complaint process. Police agencies must work with their communities to determine the best method for involving residents in the complaint process.

DISCUSSION POINTS

1. Has your department conducted a citywide survey on how residents feel about their police agency?
    - If yes, what did the agency do with the information?
    - If not, why hasn't the department engaged in this transformation process?
2. How open is your complaint process?
3. Can an individual locate the complaint process on the department's web page?
4. Does your police agency post complaint information in local areas, such as public libraries, city hall, grocery stores, schools, barber and beauty shops, and places of worship?
5. Does your agency publicly report the department's complaint process or list the type and disposition of all complaints?
6. Does your agency list all use-of-force investigations conducted by the agency? The listing should include the type of force against a person, the date of the use-of-force incident, the date of the completed investigation, the outcome of the incident, and the listing of any officer discipline.

POLICY-TRAINING-SUPERVISION-DISCIPLINE (REDIRECTION)

A well-functioning police agency will maintain and possess four key elements in its organization: policy, training, supervision, and discipline (redirection). All four elements are the key to a successful organization. All four elements must work in constant motion and continually be reviewed, enhanced, and challenged internally by the police, and the public should be involved in the process. The four elements represent the agency's ability to hold itself accountable internally with established policy, training, supervision, and discipline.

POLICY

I have learned that many police agencies lack clear and distinguishable department policies. Managing the department's policies is a challenging issue within an agency. The agency must be committed to having an in-house dedicated individual who can develop the department's policies. Many agencies are small, but can and should dedicate an individual to draft and review agency policies. Some agencies purchase off-the-shelf policy programs. Unfortunately, the canned programs do not fit every police agency. If the agency decides to purchase an off-the-shelf policy program, it should still review it and ensure the policies align with its agency and state laws. At least on an annual basis, an agency should review all policies and ensure they reflect current laws and enhanced law enforcement practices and procedures. An agency can benefit from hiring a part-time policy expert for a small fee to ensure department policies are current and reflect national generally accepted policing practices.

TRAINING

A police organization must maintain strong constitutional supportive policies covering all aspects of the law. The agency will need to train its officers on the various policies and ensure officers and police personnel are competent and skilled in carrying out the agency policies. Training officers is an important function of a police organization, and officers must maintain a strong skill set in the areas of effective communication and human dynamics. First and foremost, you should have a competent and well-versed policing expert as a department trainer. Department trainers should be characters of high quality and ensure they carry out the department's mission. Trainers cannot and should not insert their personal agenda when training officers.

SUPERVISION

Strong and highly-competent supervision is required for an agency to maintain excellence. Supervisors are the backbone of a police agency and are the closest to those who carry out the daily functions of policing. Supervisors need and must be trained in all agency policies and ensure they not only understand the policies and how they work but ensure their subordinate officers are executing the policies on a daily basis. Adhering to policies, training, and supervision results in the police organization's ability to deliver effective service. Otherwise, the employee or those impacted by police service will receive inadequate and less than professional police action. Unfortunately, many police organizations believe a good officer/investigator will make a good supervisor.

I have witnessed mistakes in promoting an officer/investigator into a supervisory role when they do not have the appropriate skill set, sometimes creating a disaster. Placing an officer/investigator into a supervisory role just because they are a good officer/investigator often disrupts an organization. Placing the individual into a supervisory role often results in what we know as the Peter Principle. Organizations have made mistakes by pushing an employee into a supervisory role, then recognizing the failure but doing nothing about making adjustments. Often and more confounding is continually promoting the individual higher, thinking the person will change. An effective promotional system to gauge and assess human behaviors, personality, and skills to function in a supervisory role are very important for agencies to maintain.

DISCIPLINE (RE-DIRECTION)

One of the most challenging aspects of police management is the area of discipline. Most supervisors hesitate to actively manage discipline with their subordinate officers. Several reasons prevent police organizations from minimizing their litigation costs and ensuring their organization is well-run by an effective disciplinary process. Far too often in my police career, I have seen firsthand how supervisors failed to actively manage their subordinate officers. First, discipline does not solely consist of suspending an officer. Discipline is a constructive mechanism that aims to align officer behavior with the agency's mission, vision, and rules of conduct.

Far too often in my years as chief, I would review a serious police allegation investigation and learn the officer had prior issues, which suddenly were brought to the attention of command staff. I remember an officer with a drinking problem whose off-duty conduct resulted in serious issues and a violation of department policy. During the internal investigation, I learned many personnel knew the officer had a drinking issue. Many officers commented about the officer's off-duty consumption of alcohol, but rarely did I hear how those same officers could have and should have intervened to assist the officer. It is easier to say nothing and go along with the flow than attempt to assist a fellow officer. Far too many careers and disruptions occurred over the years with officer behavior, resulting in investigations, suspensions, and termination from duty.

At the same time, when supervisors report alleged police misconduct to their superiors, the bosses need to take action. For example, a serious criminal incident occurred involving an investigator. One of the responding investigators had alcohol on his breath and appeared intoxicated. The investigator responded in an official police vehicle, armed with a firearm and intoxicated. The actions of the investigator were reported through the chain of command. The chain of command indicated they would take care of the issue, which was never addressed, let alone the investigator receiving any discipline or at least some alcohol counseling. Far too often, police officers have been afforded special treatment. They would have been cited and arrested for their criminal conduct if they were civilians. When police personnel observe the inability of police bosses not to take action against subordinates, it leaves a lasting impression on others in the organization of the lack of respect toward the police bosses. The police boss may be considered "one of the guys" for allowing his chosen few to slide. Still, the rest of the police organization observed the boss's inability to lead effectively.

During their time managing their officers, many police supervisors and managers have been afforded training on how to ensure their employees align with agency policy. Many attend department in-service training and receive additional emphasis in this area with continual workshops and symposiums. At times, I would call the following situation a conundrum to effective police discipline.

My agency collective bargaining unit consisted of officers and sergeants. The sergeants were in the same union as their subordinate officers, meaning the sergeant who disciplines their subordinate officer would most likely have the same union attorney and union steward representing the disciplined officer in any arbitration process. I often witnessed the lack of a sergeant to discipline an officer unless the matter was of serious police misconduct. Thus, the supervisor did not take the opportunity to coach, mentor, and, if needed, effectuate discipline. The sergeants missed opportunities to correct behaviors because of their closeness to the officer and their same union representation. Can you imagine a sergeant taking on the union in a disciplinary matter, costing the time, money, and effort of the very union that represents you? Sorry, but this didn't occur in my agency. At times, I felt bad for the sergeants as they were in what I call a "trick box." At the same time, the sergeants were not forced into their supervisory role. You see, it takes courage and leadership to be an effective supervisor. At times, you must do the right thing at the right time for the right reasons. Unfortunately, too many supervisors over my career lacked the fortitude to do this at the risk of being chastised and cast away by the rank and file.

After witnessing this conundrum over the years, few sergeants have been able to step out and call balls and strikes. It is far too easy to get along than to call out one of your subordinate officers for alleged police misconduct. Most supervisors were reluctant to go through the disciplinary process, including an arbitration hearing. I sat through enough arbitration hearings to gain a very good understanding of the police culture, specifically when it came to discipline.

Policing is a culture within itself. Many police organizations isolate themselves from the city they police, and much of this is the root cause of tension in police-community relations. Just take some time and do some research. Assess those cities that have an indifferent relationship with their police department. Some will say, "Well, it is a liberal city that caters to the poor and left-wing-minded people." I know several liberal cities with strong bonds between residents and police agencies. The liberal left-wing position is a red herring. Dig a little deeper, and one will soon discover some "we versus them" mentality approach with policing in some of the most controversial cities where the police and community just don't get along.

It takes strong police leadership to determine the root causes of police-community tensions. It takes strong police leadership to provide support for our police officers in their day-to-day work. At the same time, it takes strong leadership to provide counseling and discipline for those officers who fail to follow the department's standards and some who are involved in police misconduct. Discipline is an important and needed component in a police organization. Discipline ensures the actions of the organization are assessed for realignment of service. Discipline is often perceived as negative, but it should be an opportunity for self-correction for the employee to receive appropriate training, counseling, or a form of stricter discipline to redevelop the employee. When you hear a police agency report to the public that they have gone years without a discipline issue or grievance from the union, be cautiously aware of probable coziness between management and the union.

DISCUSSION POINTS

1. Does your police agency maintain up-to-date and legally defensible policies?
2. Is the community involved in department policy development?
3. How often do your officers train on defensive tactics, use of force, police pursuits, and de-escalation techniques?
4. Have your supervisors been trained on the core elements of supervision: legal, administrative, and operational functions?
5. What is your agency's disciplinary process? Is there a written policy? How often do you train on the policy?
6. What systems are in place to ensure your disciplinary process aligns with twenty-first-century policing practices? How does your process align with acceptable human resource management standards?
7. How do you process repetitive disciplinary issues?

SEX AND POLICING

Over my years as a police officer and police chief, I was stunned by the number of police officers who engaged in sexual encounters and used their power as police officers to intimidate others for sexual events. I was perplexed by the number of incidents where officers used their power to engage in sexual activity.

Chiefs must ensure all anonymous and signed complaints of sexual activity are investigated. Police departments should consider conducting quality control checks on officer activity. Randomly checking body-worn cameras and in-car videos is a simple method of auditing police behaviors. Reviewing and verifying officer activity sheets to their 911 computer-generated logs will confirm if the appropriate activity is noted. Police officers have an enormous amount of discretionary time during their daily work. Most officers honor their oath of office and take great pride in providing professional police service to their communities. Unfortunately, there is a small group of police officers who take advantage of opportunities to tarnish their badge and, most of all, make policing look bad. Fellow officers and supervisors are either aware or know the officers are breaking the rules and regulations. There has to be a time in the policing industry when the bad guys fear the good guys as opposed to the current dilemma in policing—the bad officers threaten the good guys for fear of retribution, shame, and being considered a rat. Our industry will continue to maintain problems and struggles with legitimacy and trust unless police officers police themselves and hold their fellow officers accountable for misdeeds.

Lastly, complete an administrative investigation on all noted sexual activity. The administrative investigation will assess and determine if other officers may be involved in this activity.

DISCUSSION POINTS

1. Conduct a thorough inquiry into all alleged police misconduct complaints.
2. Ensure all inquiries are concluded with a report or notes on what was completed.
3. Assess, review, and inquire into all department databases and communication devices for non-police-related communication between those allegedly involved in sexual misconduct.

USE OF FORCE

Use of force is a major component of a police organization. In fact, many police civil litigation lawsuits center around police use of force. Police officers tend to risk their lives and the lives of residents with use of force when there is a lack of a comprehensive structure to manage force. Unfortunately, some police agencies do not possess the ability to manage police use of force, and regrettably, at times, it takes criminal and civil intervention to control and manage a police department's use of force.

I look back over the years and cannot remember the department providing any training when patrol officers assisted in executing drug warrants. The drug location was often fortified with steel bars at the entrance doors. Drug dealers did not want the police entering without removing the bars while simultaneously fending off possible rip-offs from competing drug dealers. It was a challenge to enter, and at times, the drug unit brought along their battery ram, which was a large, heavy, and long device similar to an overweight and elongated bowling ball that would be slammed against a door to make entry. I can remember the sound the battery ram made when slammed against the door by the drug investigators. Once entering, large, angry dogs would often come running toward the door at us. I remember a drug investigator shooting at dogs running at officers after a door was rammed, kicked, and entered. This was a concerning event, especially when your day-to-day job did not involve drug work or executing search warrants. Over the years, many of us were lucky to have not been seriously injured by gunfire or an angry dog. When entering most of these locations, officers were actively pointing their firearms in the direction of the individuals inside. Establishing department policy and training on entering the drug house should have been in place to protect officers, civilians, and the department. Police policy and training are essential elements of a force management system.

POLICY

Frequently, many police agencies do not possess a principled use-of-force policy, which reflects the Constitution of the United States, particularly the elements of *Graham v. Connor* and *Tennessee v. Garner*—the standards for assessing and evaluating force along with other court decisions. Many police department policies do not contain specific language on how use of force should be used and the limitations. Additionally, many police use-of-force policies lack clear definitions, how force should be applied, and language regarding the parallel between force and the Constitution's Fourth Amendment. The Fourth Amendment is often overlooked by police agencies, as they believe the Fourth Amendment simply pertains to search and seizure. Many use-of-force policies are void of the timing of officer intervention and dealing with the mentally ill and those with other disabilities.

The department should ensure its use-of-force policy contains specific language of the officer's force that is objectively reasonable to effectively bring an incident under control while protecting the safety of other officers and civilians. The department's use-of-force policy should provide definitions for the following terms:

- deadly force
- use of force
- less-lethal force
- objectively reasonable
- serious use of force
- de-escalation
- choke hold
- warning shots
- duty to intervene
- excited delirium

Each of these definitions is important for a police use-of-force policy and should be clearly defined in the policy. Train officers on the definitions and hold officers and supervisors responsible for adhering to the policy.

The policy should define the various use-of-force levels and how these types of force are reported, investigated, and managed. Many agencies use three to four use-of-force levels. The lowest level uses of force include pointing a firearm, hand control, and noncompliant handcuffing. Mid-level uses of force include takedown, chemical spray, and electronic control deployment. Lastly, the more serious uses of force include striking someone's head with an object, a police shooting, a K9 bite, and an individual requiring medical assistance from a police encounter. Serious use-of-force incidents involve the highest level of scrutiny and investigation.

TRAINING

Training is an often overlooked aspect of a police agency. Often, a law enforcement agency will succumb to municipal financial difficulties and look to training as a method to balance a budget. Most of the time, city hall bureaucrats look at training as the fat cat and easy to cut. Many city hall number crunchers are rarely subpoenaed, required to provide a deposition, or testify to why an officer did not receive adequate training. The law enforcement agency often cuts its training budget to meet a budget deficit. This action is unwise and often will lead to potential officer safety and civil liability issues within a law enforcement agency.

I vividly remember when an officer screwed up something that supervisors referred the officer to training. This was often the quick and easy way to get rid of an issue, and the subordinate's supervisor did not have to address the deficiency. It was much easier for the supervisor to kick the ball down the street than to address the issue. To address the deficiency issue, the supervisor would have to spend time with the officer, analyze the issue, devise an action plan, and assess if the plan modified a new performance outcome. This takes work and effort, and most importantly, the supervisor will have to "get into the weeds" with the officer and their behaviors. It may not be a training issue, but that the officer is not sure of the process, is lazy, takes the easy path, and does just enough to get by. The supervisor often realizes this issue, but rather than take it on directly, the supervisor passes the problem to training—the path of least resistance.

A robust and mature police law enforcement agency will ensure its training functions are maintained well and can withstand civil litigation. An agency should ensure the following occurs:

USE-OF-FORCE TRAINING. Initial recruit required post-state training should consist of at least four weeks of training and cover topics, such as constitutional law and specifically the Fourth Amendment dealing with the seizure of a person; application and proficiency of all force tools: handgun, long gun, pepper spray, baton, controlled electrical weapon, handcuffs, and all other equipment an officer carries on their gun belt. Every force tool carried on an officer's belt should be covered under a department policy—proficiency in carrying the tool and yearly qualification. Officers should receive special training emphasizing officers intervening when force is not necessary and when to stop using force, with a focus on dealing with the mentally ill and those with disabilities.

De-escalation is often an overlooked issue of a use-of-force incident. De-escalation may mean different things to different people with different outcomes. It is imperative to establish an agency working definition. At a minimum, de-escalation should contain, assess, evaluate, and ensure the officer considered other options (when possible) than the force they use to overcome the subject. Some situations will prevent officers from utilizing any de-escalation opportunities. From my professional experience and review of hundreds of use-of-force incidents, officers have an opportunity to consider de-escalation opportunities before using force. Most use-of-force incidents involve low-level force encounters with officers and provide an opportunity for the officer to seek and consider other less-force opportunities. Considering less-force options is not admitting something wrong from the officer's perspective. The consideration is an opportunity to assess and evaluate if the officer should have or could have considered less force with what was presented at the time of the force.

Police personnel are one of the most valuable assets to an organization and, at the same time, one of the most expensive elements. I often witnessed firsthand how police supervisors lacked the wisdom and fortitude to value employees by discussing their performance in a positive manner. I experienced supervisors who would rather look the other way than confront a personnel issue. The issue was perceived as negative and personally attacking to the employee. Our organization disvalued the opportunity to improve one's behavior for far too long. Many supervisors forgot their oath of office and who they ultimately served—the public. The public expected professional police service from police officers. The public expected supervisors to coach, motivate, and positively counsel police officers. Not addressing the issue simply reinforced to the officer that they did nothing wrong.

Lastly, police agencies overlook the yearly review process of assessing current use-of-force policies and how they relate and conform to laws and industry standards. Police should review and assess their use-of-force policies annually to ensure compliance with applicable laws and training. Much like an accreditation process, annual reviews will ensure a police agency is adhering to current standards of law and incorporating proven practices in the policing profession.

DISCUSSION POINTS

1. Does the police department have a use-of-force policy that covers de-escalation, intervening, and principles of dealing with the mentally ill and those suffering from disabilities?
2. How often is the department's use-of-force policy reviewed?
3. Is the policy available to the public?
4. Does the department provide an annual use-of-force report on the number of force encounters with individuals by identifying the subject of force by race, gender, and ethnicity?
5. Are force encounters mapped out by the geographic area of your city?
6. How many excessive force complaints are made on an annual basis?
7. Of those excessive use-of-force complaints, how many are sustained, not-sustained, exonerated, and unfounded?
8. How are repeat officers who use force managed?
9. Does your department utilize an early warning system? If so, what do you know about it?
10. How often does your department require officers to qualify with firearms?

SUPERVISION

Supervision is essential for an effective law enforcement agency. Supervision provides the backbone for the agency's mission, vision, and core values and ensures personnel carry out their obligations. Certainly, a police chief can set the standards for the agency, but the first-line supervisors are the real drivers and enforcers. The supervisors interact, communicate, and establish rapport with those who do the work—the agency's officers. It is paramount and of utmost importance that first-line supervisors provide clear, precise, and energetic opportunities to subordinate officers. The front-line supervisor is essential for the agency to reach its full potential. Far too often, police personnel are promoted to a first-line supervisor position, and after a few months, they discover they are uncomfortable approaching difficult situations. I often remember new sergeants and lieutenants who were the first line of management in difficult positions because they truly had no idea how challenging being a supervisor or manager was in a law enforcement agency. Supervision can make or break a police organization and especially in force management. A police supervisor is an essential and required component in a use-of-force incident.

A supervisor is the primary and first-ranking officer who responds to a use-of-force incident. The supervisor responds to the force incident and assesses it for agency practice and policy appropriateness. The department's supervisor is responsible for ensuring agency policies are conducted per established protocol. A sound and principled supervisor will ensure the initial incident investigation is managed well.

One of the impediments and downfalls for those to effectively serve as a first-line supervisor or first-line manager is the reluctance to hold subordinates accountable. The lack of holding subordinates accountable is often caused not by the new supervisor but rather by a systematic issue within the organization. Holding individual police personnel accountable is often difficult for individuals. At times it was difficult to educate new supervisors on how to be a supervisor as the organizational culture was stronger to resist new policies and overall reforms in the department.

Some individuals want the glory, pay, and status of a supervisor, but some lack the fortitude to hold individuals accountable. Many supervisors want to be liked and placed in the best image within an agency. Holding someone accountable is not the most popular thing to do and will often cause tension and resentment in those police agencies, which have a history of not holding individuals accountable. The culture in some police agencies can be strong, with an emphasis on ensuring your place at the grill at police outings with those you used to manage after you've retired. If the organization's leader and the agency realize the importance of self-reflection and re-direction, it would be much easier for law enforcement supervisors and managers to impose discipline on subordinate employees.

I remember an investigator conducting suspect interviews incorrectly and their supervisor counseling them to do better in future interviews. The investigator did not adhere to their supervisor's counseling session and repeated the same behavior. The supervisor again counseled the investigator and sought their commander's assistance for direction. The commander kicked the can down the street and avoided supporting the supervisor on how to redirect the investigator. The commander avoided the confrontation and told the supervisor to let it go. Not only was the action outside any industry management protocol, but it empowered the investigator and lessened the ability of the sergeant to manage their subordinate personnel. After a while, supervisors who work under that leadership style will shut down and just show up for their eight hours of work and not manage their personnel.

I often heard there was no reason to supervise when subordinate officers and investigators could simply do an end-run to the supervisor's commander over issues. I often heard and witnessed supervisors who were not backed by their commanders who caved to the masses over disciplinary issues. I often witnessed officers going directly to a commander, who would ultimately overturn a supervisor's initial decision. I realize there are times when a supervisor or commander will get it wrong. Still, I witnessed line officers and investigators going directly to their commander and second-guessing their immediate supervisor's decision.

SUPERVISOR TRAINING

New supervisory training is important in ensuring the supervisor is well-trained before assessing subordinate behaviors. Supervisor training should consist of an initial supervisory school. The initial opportunity should allow the soon-to-be promoted or aspiring supervisor to seek out and observe supervisory activities prior to their promotion. Far too often, supervisors take a promotional test, and they are eventually promoted off of the list to their newly established supervisory position. This could be in a police or jail supervisory capacity. The person is most likely the best qualified and deserves the promotion, but their new position is much different than their current assignment. Many police agencies place the newly promoted supervisor with another working and fellow supervisor for a few days in what some consider a shadowing opportunity. The shadowing opportunity allows the newly promoted supervisor to work alongside a current supervisor for a few days or weeks before being sent out on their own.

I remember my initial training after being promoted to sergeant. I shadowed a senior sergeant on the patrol shift. I don't fault the sergeant who allowed me to shadow along with a ten-hour shift. We went on a few calls and experienced some interactions in the few days of our partnership. A few years after my experience with the shadow event of 1995, in 2006, I established a formal supervisory opportunity for new supervisors and current commanders to learn more about operations and the department's administrative functions.

New supervisors and commanders and non-sworn supervisory staff were delegated to several supervisory extended courses dealing with human behaviors, negative employees, staffing, discipline, technology, and how to motivate subordinates. Equally, I discovered many new supervisors and commanders lacked experience with many of the organization's administrative functions, particularly Internal Affairs. Far too often, someone would call the patrol shift commander and make a minor complaint against an officer. Patrol would often transfer the complaint to Internal Affairs. This process was flawed in many ways. First, minor complaints could often be processed at the shift level without the involvement of Internal Affairs. Rude behavior and not properly investigating a crime incident were two of the most frequent complaints. The patrol shift could and should be handling those types of complaints. If a supervisor is responsible for providing a comprehensive performance evaluation of their subordinate officer, then at the same time, they should be responsible for handling low-level complaints of their behaviors. However, if a complaint of a more serious nature were received, such as excessive use of force and theft, then the complaint would be investigated by Internal Affairs. The department provided training to new supervisors and commanders on how to manage the complaint process along with factors associated with the collective bargaining units and department rules and regulations.

At the time of my appointment as police chief, as an agency, we established areas that we should and could improve. We implemented at least two weeks of supervisory indoctrination of the agency policies, practices, and operations. The new supervisors met and engaged in an adult learning environment, allowing new supervisors to converse, ask questions, and challenge what they were expected to do in the coming weeks. At the same time, new managers were expected to work alongside assigned commanders in administrative and internal investigations. Exposing existing and new managers in Internal Affairs allowed personnel to learn city administrative rules and procedures and gain additional opportunities to learn about personnel human resource management.

Implementing training opportunities within the organization was important for all new and current supervisors and commanders. Cops are hired as police officers to enforce the laws and regulations of a city. Cops are not hired to be supervisors and commanders. It is essential for police chiefs to recognize the differences between a street cop and a manager of street cops. Over my tenure, we provided many opportunities for new and current supervisors and commanders to excel in their management of subordinate employees.

DISCUSSION POINTS

1. What opportunities are set in your agency to allow interested personnel to learn about supervisory and manager roles?

2. Do you allow current supervisors and managers to shadow areas of your agency that have limited exposure? For instance, if a patrol sergeant is interested in transferring to an investigative supervisory role, do you allow the individual to shadow the investigative area and learn firsthand their operations?

3. Do you have a formal training curriculum set for new supervisory and management personnel?

USE-OF-FORCE REVIEW BOARD

An essential function of use-of-force management is the Use-of-Force Review Board. At the conclusion of a serious use-of-force incident, the Use-of-Force Review Board assesses the final work product of the incident and decides the outcome in terms of policy, tactics, and training. The Use-of-Force Review Board does not necessarily initiate discipline stemming from the incident, but rather focuses on the "systems" of the use-of-force incident. After a use-of-force incident, supervisors may determine policy violations. This is the time for initiating an investigation before the case goes to the Use-of-Force Review Board.

Many police agencies do not utilize a Use-of-Force Review Board to determine if policy, tactics, and training were followed within the use-of-force incident. Agencies are indifferent to this practice for several reasons. First, some agencies believe that if you expose deficiencies in the use-of-force incident, you expose yourself to civil litigation and just assist the defense. This assertion is untrue and far from the very reasons to conduct such reviews. Once a use-of-force incident is over—it is over. There is no way to go back and unwind the use-of-force incident. For example, if the shooting appears out of policy, there is no way to go back and change what occurred. If an officer used excessive force and caused severe injuries to someone, then there is no way to go back and make the injuries disappear. Similarly, an airplane crash is an unfortunate incident, as is a medical procedure when a doctor makes a mistake. Both incidents involve human factors and humans making choices, which might not be aligned with proper procedures. You cannot unwind an airplane crash or re-do a medical procedure when there is a catastrophic loss. Airline and medical industries treat such incidents as system errors, which require a holistic approach to determine what factors caused the system error. Likewise, police departments should model and learn from the airline and medical systems approach in determining how use-of-force incidents may have had a different outcome with a rigorous review of the incident.

Secondly, and most importantly, reviewing a use-of-force incident is hard work, and the accountability factor is again inserted in such a review. Examining a use-of-force incident requires police personnel to review subordinate actions and, at times, tell fellow officers they could have used other force options; they didn't need to use the force they used; the officer tactics were outside of standard policy and training. Calling out fellow officers is not popular, but it saves lives, protects innocent individuals, and saves police careers. My experience designing, training, and implementing use-of-force review boards is essential to a police agency. Using force against someone is authorized by police officers under law and policy. At the same time, a thorough review is essential for such incidents to ensure the law and agency protocols are aligned with the use of force.

The composition of the Use-of-Force Review Board is important. An agency should ensure all voices of the department are heard in assessing the use-of-force incident. The following are personnel who should be part of the Use-of-Force Review Board:

- At least an odd number of senior-ranking members of the department for voting purposes. The odd-number senior-ranking members of the department are the voting members.
- Other non-voting members of the board should include a tactical and training officer, the bargaining unit member's representative, and corporation counsel.

DISCUSSION POINTS

1. Does your agency have an established Use-of-Force Review Board?
2. Who are the members of the board?
3. How are the members trained?
4. How does an agency ensure board recommendations such as policy, training, and equipment are followed up and implemented?
5. How are agency officers trained with any of the recommendations?

INTERNAL USE-OF-FORCE AUDITING

An integral and final component of a force management process is internal auditing. The purpose of internal auditing is to confirm that the agency follows departmental policies throughout the use-of-force incident. The auditing should be conducted by someone or a unit not involved in any aspect of the use-of-force incident. Some agencies have external auditing systems, which conduct departmental auditing of multiple issues of an agency. Some agencies conduct an audit after a high-profile incident, which has caused concern and community tension with the police department. A department should perform ongoing use-of-force audits to ensure compliance per established agency policy.

Additionally, an agency is urged to assess other areas of their organization, which may lead to unreported uses of force. For example, agencies consider auditing injury to suspects, resisting arrest, and obstructing incidents as another method of auditing to determine any unreported uses of force. In the rollout of body-worn cameras (BWC), agencies have set up audit processes to assess a certain number of BWCs to determine if there are any unreported use-of-force incidents, along with validating officer conduct with department policies.

DISCUSSION POINTS

1. Does your agency have an internal/external audit process?

2. What types of police actions are being audited?

3. Does the agency publicly report internal audit results?

EARLY WARNING SYSTEM

I remember a complaint from a person who felt the officer had used coarse language and excessive force when addressing the individual. The individual wanted to sign a complaint against the officer. I asked Internal Affairs what prior complaints the officer had. The officer did not have many years on the job, and I was briefed the officer had an excessive number of complaints of rude behavior and excessive force. All of the complaints were either unfounded or exonerated. I was taken aback by the number of complaints for such a young officer and discovered that no remedial action was taken to address any of the issues with the officer. Although all allegations were unfounded or exonerated, how could one officer, especially a fairly young and new officer, have a consistent number of similar complaints?

I pondered how the officer's supervisors and commanders were unaware of the officer's behaviors. How could this officer operate in such a silo and no direct supervisor? You see, addressing an officer who is young in his career where something is wrong but is viewed as okay by your organization will be seen as a betrayal of the system. You will likely be looked at as some crusader and out of touch with the tough streets the officers have to work. What does the administration or "white shirts" know about policing? Anyone who dares to question the tactics and maneuvers of officers is simply a "Monday night quarterback," or you become a "my way or the highway" authoritarian. So, you see, you can go along to get along, and you will be fine. Many people will enjoy your company, you will be looked at from the line as a "cop's cop," and you will be thought of as "one of the guys." You may also want to consider the longer you allow the continuance of bad behavior without addressing it, the more difficult it will be to deal with in the future. "Why now, Chief, do you want to address an issue when you have allowed the same behavior to occur in the past and said nothing?" No one said it would be easy to be the chief. Organizational culture is very difficult to change, and it takes many years to overcome the past. As the chief of police, you will have little choice but to challenge the rank and file, challenge the organizational culture, and do what is right for effective civil rights for all. If you choose to go along with the current culture or provide the excuse, "That's the way we have always done it," you will be setting yourself up for severe personal and professional damage. You will likely face a lawsuit, deposition, civil rights violation, or investigative inquiry about why you responded the way you did. Are you willing to open your agency up to a lawsuit out of ignorance just to get along? Are you willing to open up your city and police agency to a large monetary award because you, as chief of police, failed to do what you pledged to do with the oath of office you swore to uphold?

I worked with the city's corporation counsel and the union's cooperation in addressing the fairly new officer with several complaints. As a result of the officer's actions, the department implemented an early warning system, which tracks officers' specific liability and risk incidents. The early warning system (EWS) captures officers' behaviors and actions before they become too severe of a liability issue. Discipline is not simply punitive but should also allow for the officer to re-tool. You see, an agency's biggest and most expensive asset is its people. We need to ensure, as police executives, that we do everything we can to foster care and compassion for our personnel. At times, being the chief of police is like a parent, and in this case, a father who looks over and tends to those who need mentoring, counseling, and discipline at times. The sole purpose of the EWS is to manage behaviors. EWS does not look into every risk issue but tracks and scores the risk components.

The EWS was a great benefit for the department. For example, review the chart below. Conceptually, most early warning systems are similar and capture "police risk behaviors." The behaviors are those incidents that the department and officer should be concerned about. The chart includes three officers: Adam, Baker, and Charlie. The department has decided over a rolling six-month period that an officer cannot have two or more use-of-force incidents; two or more citizen complaints; two or more internal complaints; or two or more pursuit incidents. The department determined in the same rolling six-month period that an officer cannot have a combination of three or more of the four behaviors.

During the rolling six-month period, the following number of incidents and associated colors represent the following:

GREEN = NO ACTIVITY
YELLOW = 1 BEHAVIOR
RED = 2 BEHAVIORS

During the six months, Officer Adam had one use-of-force incident, zero citizen complaints, zero internal complaints, and one pursuit. The total score is two for the rolling six-month period.

During the six months, Officer Baker had zero use-of-force incidents, one citizen complaint, zero internal complaints, and zero pursuits. The total score is one for the rolling six-month period.

During the six months, Officer Charlie had two use-of-force incidents, two citizen complaints, zero internal complaints, and zero pursuits. The total score is four for the rolling six-month period.

OFFICER	USE OF FORCE	CITIZEN COMPLAINT	INTERNAL COMPLAINT	PURSUIT	OVERALL
ADAM					2
BAKER					1
CHARLIE					4

Anytime you score a single behavior in the red or an overall score of red, a supervisor will receive an alert. The supervisor assesses the behaviors of the officer—what might be causing the high number of risks. The supervisor does not make any determinations on the actual incidents, just the behavior itself. For example, Officer Charlie's supervisor does not determine anything about the use-of-force and citizen complaint incidents but rather what might be causing the increase. A separate and distinct investigation takes place for the use-of-force and citizen complaint incidents.

Officer Charlie's supervisor reviews the behaviors and may decide some coaching, one-on-one mentoring, or in-service training may assist Officer Charlie. Whatever the supervisor determines, a meeting is held with the officer, and a discussion about the behaviors takes place. Once a plan of action is determined, the supervisor types the action and ensures the officer receives the appropriate redirection. In the end, the department is focused on lessening the number of behaviors and redirecting the officer to a better outcome. The demands and stress of a police officer are great, and we need to ensure we have the correct systems and processes in place to protect our valued asset—our people—and at the same time, ensure officers are treating residents with respect and professionalism.

DISCUSSION POINTS

1. Does your police agency maintain an early warning system?
2. If so, what kind of system? If the agency does not maintain an early warning system, what process is in place to manage behaviors?
3. Does your chief of police publicly address the system and how it is working without providing specific officer names?
4. How are supervisors trained on how to manage the process with subordinate officers?

INTERNAL AFFAIRS

If you want to gauge an agency's sincerity toward constitutional and professional policing, look at who is assigned to manage the Internal Affairs investigation process. I know some very good and dedicated police professionals in our industry who did a very fine job assigned as the "palace guard" for the agency's integrity. I am also aware of and have observed firsthand those chiefs of police who assign weak-minded and mediocre police supervisors to Internal Affairs. However, if you assign an individual to one of the most important functions of a police agency that lacks the ability to investigate their own, then the police chief has accomplished their goal: they most likely will not come up with thorough investigations, and most of the complaints will either be unfounded or exonerated. Unfortunately, some police chiefs want this practice and outcome as they do not have to contend with any strife in the organization and special interest groups. Additionally, I know chiefs of police who ensure some alleged complaints do not get investigated due to the chief's friendships with other officers and special interest groups.

Internal affairs are an important aspect of your role as chief of police. One of the areas to manage effectively is the complaint process. After my appointment as chief, I realized there was a high number of complaints classified as "failed to file," which means someone complained to the police department about an alleged police misconduct violation against a police officer. This alleged complaint could be anything from rude behavior of an officer, abusive use of police power, to excessive use of force. Normally, the complainant comes to the police station and speaks with the commander of the Internal Affairs division. The commander would listen to the complainant and then provide a written complaint form for the complainant to complete. Most of the time, the complainant would take the form and want to go home and consult with their attorney or family member before completing and returning the form. Our department completes an annual report highlighting the agency's performance for the past year. I reviewed a chart depicting the number of failed-to-file complaints over seven years. Some years would have double-digit numbers of individuals who did not return their signed complaints. Graph 1 depicts the Rockford Police Department Excessive Use-of-Force Complaints from 2004 to 2010.

GRAPH 1

ROCKFORD POLICE DEPARTMENT EXCESSIVE USE-OF-FORCE COMPLAINTS, 2004–2010

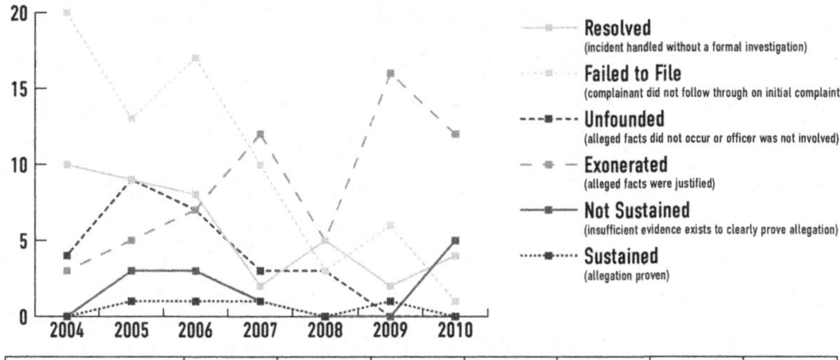

	2004	2005	2006	2007	2008	2009	2010
SUSTAINED	0	1	1	1	0	1	0
NOT SUSTAINED	0	3	3	1	0	0	5
EXONERATED	3	5	7	12	5	16	12
UNFOUNDED	4	9	8	2	5	2	4
FAILED TO FILE	20	13	17	10	3	6	1
RESOLVED	10	9	7	3	3	0	0
TOTAL	37	40	43	29	16	25	22

In 2010 the Rockford Police Department received 22 excessive force complaints. The above chart describes the outcome of these investigations, along with tracking such complaints, since 2004.

- **SUSTAINED (allegation proven)**
- **NOT SUSTAINED (insufficient evidence exists to clearly prove allegation)**
- **EXONERATED (alleged facts were justified)**
- **UNFOUNDED (alleged facts did not occur or officer was not involved)**
- **FAILED TO FILE (complainant did not follow-through on initial complaing)**
- **RESOLVED (incident handled without a formal investigation)**

From 2004 until 2007, the number of failed-to-file excessive use-of-force complaints was double-digit. In 2007, the number went from ten to three in 2008. In 2010, the number was one.

Managing use of force is an important component of an agency and must be a high priority for any police chief for the following reasons:

First, every alleged excessive use-of-force complaint made to the department is important. The department needs to determine the validity of an alleged excessive use-of-force complaint. The department needs to protect the integrity of the organization by assessing every alleged excessive use-of-force incident. If the alleged complaint is false, the person making the complaint is wrong and could be potentially charged in a criminal complaint by the prosecutor for making a false complaint. If the alleged complaint is true, the department needs to investigate and determine what occurred.

Second, the department missed an opportunity to investigate the alleged excessive use-of-force complaints that were not returned. For example, if someone made a complaint about an officer for excessive use of force, the department would not do a cursory review of what took place unless the complainant returned the complaint. This lack of initial investigation is a disservice to the officer and agency. Chiefs must attempt to review every alleged complaint and make some initial inquiry with or without a signed complaint. I remember shortly before I retired, a woman complained some officers had entered her residence regarding a warrant for her boyfriend and used excessive force. The woman stated the police officers pushed her as they entered her apartment, and she broke her tooth. We reviewed the incident and discovered our officers were not involved in the incident, but another police agency had entered the residence and made the arrest. We contacted the other agency and made them aware of the allegation. The police official responded that they would look into the matter if and when the woman came to their office. I could never understand an agency that did not at least make inquiries into alleged police misconduct prior to being served an official complaint or lawsuit. Again, this is an example of police management not wanting to learn if any of their officers were involved in an incident, which may have gone against police and procedure. Waiting for someone to complain is simply ignoring an issue, which you most likely believe will not be good for the department.

I have recently learned that some agencies who receive an alleged excessive use-of-force complaint hold the complaint in abeyance as the officer transfers to another police agency. If the agency decides to move forward and investigate the alleged complaint, the department may potentially find the force excessive or unauthorized by department policy. Now the officer who wants to transfer may not get the new job due to the excessive use-of-force complaint. On the other hand, the agency that may receive the transfer officer has a duty and responsibility to check the background of the applicant officer fully. There are ways and methods to determine the full background of the officer before hiring them. Full-signed personnel waivers for all alleged and actual complaints is one way to pour through the applicant officer's file. It is ethically wrong if the agency holds back because they don't want to hurt the officer's opportunity to move to another agency. More importantly, it opens the agency to potential civil action.

Third, the department failed to follow up with those who made an alleged complaint against an officer. The complainant failed to bring the complaint back to the police station, and the department failed to inquire with the person over the initial meeting. Was there something the department could have learned from the complaint? Was the complaint true? The complainant made the initial attempt to claim some alleged police violation. The department failed to attempt a cursory review of the incident. In the end, the complainant was not totally "heard," and the department failed to find closure.

Before my retirement, we had very few failed-to-file complaints. If someone made an alleged complaint against an officer, the department thoroughly followed up with the individual. We first attempted to make personal contact, then phone follow-up, and lastly, a certified letter to the initial complainant stating we would like to hear from them. After this, we discontinued communication with the person. If the department feels there is enough information for a formal complaint, then the complaint is handled or at least handled on the shift level as an inquiry. In the end, complaints must be taken seriously, and a police chief must ensure they have a sound, principled, and fair complaint process. Every police agency needs to protect the reputation of the agency along with protecting officers. At the same time, we must hold the mirror in front of us and be able to maintain a level of self-critical analysis and make wrongs correct in our profession. If warranted, there is no room for police violations that impede the freedoms of constitutional policing.

Any alleged police misconduct requires an internal investigation to determine what the officer did during their alleged police misconduct. During the investigation, it may become known that other police personnel were involved in the police misconduct. The investigation may also determine whether the agency may want to enhance a policy, training, or protocol. Far too often, police chiefs allow the involved officer to retire, and the matter just disappears, resulting in no internal investigation being conducted. Making a decision not to conduct an internal investigation places a stain on the police department and hampers the ability of the agency to determine if there are other bad apples in the organization.

Lastly, I believe many police chiefs error grossly when confronted with an officer who may have committed criminal conduct or is being investigated for it. For example, an off-duty officer is drinking at a local cop bar and decides to play pool with some fellow officers. While playing pool, an individual wants the pool table, and the officers tell the individual they are still playing. The individual cannot take no for an answer, and one of the officers strikes the individual over the head with a pool cue. The individual is injured, and the cops leave the bar. The individual complains about the incident, and the officer who struck the individual complains about the assault. A criminal investigation is conducted, and the district attorney formally charges the officer. The police chief places the officer on administrative duty, which means the officer is stripped of their police duties and would normally be assigned to their residence until the completion of the criminal process. At this point, many police chiefs fail in their ability to police their agency.

First, many police chiefs will not begin an internal investigation into the officer's conduct because of the criminal process. These are some of the reasons you will hear from police chiefs who delay the internal investigation:

Chiefs do not want to jeopardize the internal compelled interview. Public employees, particularly police officers who are the focus of a department violation and complaint, can be forced to provide testimony to their involvement in the incident. The internal compelled statement cannot be used for any criminal purposes. This is a weak argument for the following reason: if an officer has been formally criminally charged and arrested, then one will presume a criminal investigation occurred, and police investigators took the time to interview the victim of the crime, other witnesses to the incident (police officers), forensic evidence, and any other film footage. The officer may have provided a statement or refused a criminal interview. The district attorney has all of the required information to move forward and have a trial. Delaying the compelled interview has no bearing on the criminal incident. Waiting months and years to conduct an administrative compelled investigation just allows individuals to forget what occurred and allows potential witnesses to ensure their stories are aligned.

DISCUSSION POINTS

1. All alleged serious police conduct requires an administrative review or internal investigation.

2. Does your police agency make available data to the public on the number of complaints and outcomes?

3. Does your department investigate matters even though the employee may retire during the initial inquiry?

4. Who will you assign to manage your Internal Affairs section? What skill set do they possess in this complex and sensitive component of the department?

5. Consider taking newly promoted first-line supervisors to shadow the lead person in your Internal Affairs section. Place the newly appointed supervisor in Internal Affairs for at least sixty days. This temporary assignment will allow the newly appointed supervisor to gain a perspective on the mechanics of IA.

6. Consider placing mid-level supervisors in IA for at least one year. This will allow the mid-level supervisor an opportunity to appreciate the functions of IA. The year appointment will allow the newly promoted mid-level manager to work on some IA case investigations.

CIVIL LITIGATION

Many police agencies do not process, assess, and appreciate police civil litigation. Many police agencies do not receive legal counsel or engage with them regarding those who file a civil lawsuit against a police agency or police officer. As chief, I regularly met with the city's legal staff and reviewed all civil litigation claims made against the police department. I included Internal Affairs and my command staff in the regular meetings. The meetings consisted of a shared police/city legal spreadsheet containing the plaintiff's name, the date the claim was filed, the alleged action, and the status of the civil claim. Each claim was then reviewed.

The meetings were intended to determine if the claim had an associated police incident report, which means if a plaintiff filed a civil action against the department and officers, we would assess if there was a reportable use-of-force/arrest incident report. We would review any all-police reports to determine if a use of force occurred. Usually, the officer's police reports would indicate if such actions occurred. Another method to determine if force may have occurred is to review body-worn camera video (BWC). BWC footage is an excellent method to provide openness and transparency within a police agency. Likewise, squad car mobile dash video (MVU) is an additional opportunity for police agencies to record police actions.

The civil litigation review process was an excellent method to ensure the case was proceeding through the various courts in a timely manner, along with an opportunity to assess if the department's policy and training needed any enhancement. Likewise, plaintiff lawsuits were a method to evaluate the arrest or the use-of-force incident. The plaintiff's claims may have shed new information on the police officer's actions. If so, a new inquiry was made per the officer's conduct. This process often raised eyebrows from police personnel and now my work in the civil litigation arena.

First, I would be asked, "Why are we doing the work for the defense?" No, we are not doing the work of the defense; we are correcting any potential actions now instead of waiting months or years before the case makes its way to court. For example, if a policy agency recognizes the use of the Taser was out of policy and excessive against an individual, the department should take immediate action to reconcile the officer's conduct. The fact that the officer may have used excessive force is in the past, and the civil-criminal nature of the complaint will ultimately have to rectify the incident at the time of occurrence. If the department recognizes a policy, practice, or training issue with the plaintiff's information, then the agency should identify and fix the issue.

Using the same example regarding the Taser, if the officer used excessive force, which is determined through the plaintiff's lawsuit, it's in the department's best interest to fix the issue now instead of later in a potential trial. If the same officer is not counseled for their excessive force, then the agency is in a bad situation by allowing the behavior to go uncorrected. Further, if a policy is recognized as deficient during a plaintiff's lawsuit, it is best to modify it now instead of waiting months or years before it goes to trial. How many other potential plaintiffs were victimized by the same policy? How many potential plaintiffs were tased by the same officer before the trial if the agency knew there was an issue?

DISCUSSION POINTS

1. Does your agency have an established review system to assess plaintiff lawsuits?
2. Who is involved in the process?
3. What, if any, policy, training, or equipment modifications are made during the review?
4. How often does the chief of police confer with the corporation counsel regarding civil litigation?

FOOT PURSUITS

One of the most difficult policies to implement was a foot pursuit policy. Officers, supervisors, and some command staff could not understand the importance of a foot pursuit policy. I vividly remember a supervisor questioning why we would need a foot pursuit policy.

Why would we want to restrict a police officer, and isn't this just letting the bad guys go? The challenge of this policy was to focus on the safety of officers and others during a foot pursuit. We ultimately created this policy after a review of several police incidents where officers placed themselves in great danger while pursuing individuals. The following are some events I recalled while researching the need for a foot pursuit policy:

An officer attempted to make a traffic stop, and the driver suddenly stopped their auto and took off running. The officer ran after the driver in the rear of residential homes, climbing fences and running around the back of homes. The officer had difficulty notifying communications of their location and the description of the subject. The officer did not know their location and was unfamiliar with the area. The officer had no idea if a dog was present in the rear of the homes, and the lighting was dim as it was late in the evening. The officer slipped and fell at one point when he had his gun unholstered and in his hand. The driver was later located and arrested for not having a valid license and resisting arrest.

In a similar example, an officer attempted to make a traffic stop, but the driver fled from their auto, and the officer pursued the driver. The officer was not familiar with the area and surroundings. The officer chased the driver for not stopping and pursued the individual for a simple traffic offense. The officer fell while chasing the driver and then got up to observe the driver holding a large stick. The officer was now confronted with the driver of an auto, who had a large stick in his hands. The officer drew their firearm and pointed it at the driver, who fled the area.

Both examples provide a dangerous situation for the officer and others. The officers in both situations made poor tactical decisions to pursue an alleged traffic offender in areas that were inherently dangerous and placed the officers in harm. Additionally, both incidents involved fellow backup officers a great distance away, with the officers unable to accurately know their location and direction of travel.

One of the last discussions before implementing the foot pursuit policy involved the pursuit of offenders. Many officers could not just let the person go, meaning officers should consider stopping a pursuit only if the risk outweighs the pursuit of a minor infraction. This discussion lasted days as many officers and supervisors felt that the bad guy was just getting away, and we (police) had a duty to pursue. This thought process was so flawed and counter to officer wellness. For so long, our organization and many police departments have placed officers in great harm and risk by pursuing low-level alleged crimes where it is just too risky to pursue someone. These were difficult conversations as the culture instilled in them to get the bad guy at any cost.

Lastly, an officer can often identify the pursuing driver with the assistance of technology and information about the auto, including their license plate and other contents in the auto. A follow-up with the auto and driver's description is a better method to eventually apprehend the driver rather than risk the officer's welfare.

DISCUSSION POINTS

1. Does your agency have a foot pursuit policy?

2. How does your agency train an officer for foot pursuits?

3. Does your agency conduct any after-action reviews of foot pursuits?

SUPERVISORY INVESTIGATION – USE OF FORCE

One of the most difficult discussions and final policy implementations involved a supervisory investigation of the use-of-force process.

In 2006, the department did not require a supervisor to respond or investigate an officer's use of force. At the time, an officer could strike an individual with their baton, discharge their Taser at an individual, or use force on someone requiring hospitalization, and none of these incidents required a supervisory response to investigation. At the time, a supervisor would simply review and sign off on the officer's criminal police report. Rarely would an officer's use of force be subjected to any further review than the initial police report.

Under most uses of force and particularly serious use-of-force incidents, the new policy required a supervisor to respond to the scene of the incident. The following were some of the required duties of the responding supervisor:

- Check on the officer/subject of force for any possible injuries.
- Summon the assistance of medical for any injured individuals.
- Confer with officers and determine what occurred.
- Confer with the subject of force and determine what occurred.
- Canvass for any non-officer witnesses to the use-of-force incident.
- Canvass for any potential security cameras in the area which would have captured the use-of-force incident.
- Secure any evidence.
- Take photographs of any complaint of injury areas or injuries.
- Complete a timely report within the established policy guidelines.

After the implementation of this policy, an individual complained that officers beat him up. The complainant made specific actions of how the officers conducted themselves against him. Due to the department's practice of implementing a supervisory investigation of force, the significant pieces of the investigation were complete. There was no need to go back out to the scene and investigate an area already investigated during the initial supervisor's response to the incident scene. The initial incident investigation captured elements of what took place: officer reports and interviews, witness canvass, and any potential evidence collection. In this complaint, a responding officer had an MVU, and the camera captured the incident with the complainant struggling with the officers. The complainant's version of what took place did not match their complaint of excessive force. The MVU and initial supervisory force investigation allowed the department to respond immediately to a high-risk event and ensure practices and policies were adhered to in the incident. Additionally, capturing the initial incident with a complete and thorough investigation prevented an additional investigation.

There was initial reluctance from supervisors to engage in this sort of investigation, but in the end, it served a very good purpose. Most importantly, if a supervisory investigation of force occurred, there was little chance a complaint investigation was needed. Internal Affairs would receive and review the complaint and allegations. Internal Affairs would then review the completed supervisory investigation to ensure it captured salient points and did not leave anything out from the complaint allegations. We wanted to ensure all allegations were addressed and covered in the initial use-of-force investigation. Most of the time, a complaint would come forward after any individual's criminal complaint was resolved. This would take, at times, months or over a year to resolve. Prior to supervisory use-of-force investigations, Internal Affairs would conduct the complaint allegation. Investigating the complaint allegation several months after the incident causes several issues. First, an individual's recall of the incident becomes vague and fades. Individuals have a difficult time remembering significant moments of a highly-charged incident. Second, physical evidence is lost or unavailable due to the time the complaint is received and the response of IA. Third, the agency loses the ability to canvass for witnesses who may have witnessed the use-of-force event. It is best to capture a witness account right after the occurrence rather than wait days and months to attempt to locate any possible witnesses.

DISCUSSION POINTS

1. Does your agency have a supervisor's use-of-force investigation policy?
2. How are supervisors trained to investigate force?
3. Are the supervisor's use-of-force investigations completed in a timely manner?

COMMUNITY RELATIONS

When you think of police-community relations, you may think of the events witnessed on television and how the community interacts with its police department. The interactions should be positive and bring out the best for the community. Unfortunately, my initial experience with community relations was diminished by an organization that treated police-community relations as secondary and not a high priority of the agency. Community relations was considered the not-so-cool thing to do, but rather an emphasis was placed on violent crime investigations and arrests. If the department had taken a larger assessment of community relations, strategies and relationship building could have been implemented to lessen the outcome of shootings and violent crime investigations.

My first experience with police-community relations was with one investigator assigned to the unit. I rarely observed the investigator interacting with the community, holding community meetings, providing positive-building relations with the community, or publicly reporting police-community relations. I am not saying the person was indifferent, but the agency did not make this a high priority and a core mission of the department. It appeared the assignment was

more of a person assigned to the position for appearances, not doing the work needed to foster stronger relationships with the community and develop strategies to lessen community tensions.

The community relations office was located in the basement of our police station. Some might say there was a space issue, but we had ample room in our building to realign and expand new offices where the public could connect with community relations. Can you imagine a community resident having to go through three layers of security to connect with a community service officer? The community service officer should have been positioned to best serve the residents of a community in a convenient location. Placing the community service officer in the lower bowels of the organization indicated the priority of the agency.

DISCUSSION POINTS

1. Do you have a community relations unit?
2. What is the purpose of the unit?
3. How is the unit connected with the community?
4. How does a community member contact the community relations unit?

FITNESS FOR DUTY

One of the areas, which has little literature and practical information for police chiefs, is the extent of fitness for duty (FFD) for police officers. My experience is that most police chiefs have very little experience in the area of FFD, and most will miss several opportunities to recognize a potential FFD. When the situation does occur, the chief will need assistance with this important issue.

An FFD is a referral to a medical or mental health provider with a license to practice in their respective fields. The purpose of an FFD referral of an officer is to gain an independent medical or psychological opinion on the status of a police officer to perform their duties. There are many stresses in the police profession. Some officers are unable to cope physically, mentally, or psychologically in the police profession for a variety of reasons. Often, an officer will experience a traumatic event while on the job, or it's also possible to have had a traumatic event prior to the job as a police officer or in their personal life. Due to the increased frequency of FFDs, an agency should have multiple systems in place to detect and assist with these mental, physical, and psychological issues. Some officers find it very difficult when they are referred for an FFD. I also found supervisors reluctant to refer a subordinate officer for an FFD. My experience is after the referral, many would discuss signs and symptoms of the officer's behavior or physical ability to perform the essential job tasks as an officer after the referral. My belief is this is another area of crossing the blue line. It's easy to sit back and watch the show instead of bringing forward an issue regarding an officer's welfare. Many in our profession support officer wellness and safety. These are essential components for the well-being of our officers. At the same time, I find it very confusing that police officers are reluctant to bring forward the safety and security issues of their fellow officers.

Far too often, referrals were made after a traumatic situation when the officer should have been referred before the current issue. In many of the FFD referrals that I approved, the officer's behavior was well observed by officers and supervisors. Officers and supervisors were reluctant to cross the line and report the officer's condition higher up the chain of command. It's easier for some in our profession to go along and not challenge the status quo to assist their fellow officer. In my tenure as police chief, I recommended over ten officers for an FFD. Most of the referrals were of my signature, and one was from a first-line supervisor. Interestingly, most police supervisors will hedge their view of someone who should be referred for an FFD. Most FFDs occur for either physical or psychological reasons. Referring someone for an FFD is not an easy decision. Still, if you are unwilling to decide to send an officer for an FFD, you should not be in a position of authority and accountability.

My initial guess is police supervisors shy away from recommending someone for an FFD. What's amazing is that most police officers rely on their fellow police officers to back them up on a "hot call," assist them on a traffic stop, get in and assist with a fight, and help put the handcuffs on someone when the fight is over. Officers and supervisors assist each other on a daily basis, and most will develop life-long friendships. Others will marry and live with each other. The closeness is real, and officers get into the personal lives of each other. Many will share their life secrets about life, marriage, relationships, stress, and anything else. At times, police officers may know more about each other than their own family or friends.

At times, police officers forget why they decided to become police officers. Some officers get jaded and feel that "those people" deserve what they get, or they deserve their situation. These officers demonstrate signs and symptoms of emotional stress, confusion, and purpose in their life. They are missing opportunities to use existing systems and processes to assist police officers who get off track. Future policing supervisors must recognize how they assist fellow officers using an FFD.

DISCUSSION POINTS

1. Does your department have a fitness for duty policy?
2. Are all personnel aware of the policy?
3. Does the department have resources available to assist officers with alcohol, drug, emotional stress, fatigue, and family counseling?

POLICING AND PORNOGRAPHY

Early in my tenure as chief of police, the department discovered police officers involved in on-duty pornography viewing. The pornography viewing was not associated with any police investigation, but rather personnel viewing pornography for their own enjoyment. Those involved in the pornography viewing were investigators, many of whom were assigned to one department area. The pornography viewing occurred during the hours the investigators were supposed to be working and investigating crimes. I heard time and again from the investigator area that they were overburdened and needed more personnel. There was just not enough time to complete case assignments, call back crime victims, and keep reports updated in the records system. I never heard from supervisors and commanders in the investigator area about how much time the investigators spent viewing pornography. I never heard how that lost and unused time would have provided them more personnel resource time to work cases, solve crimes, and keep crime victims updated with their crime incidents.

Viewing pornography on duty at taxpayer cost was another issue, but the larger problem was how could a small group of investigators in a certain area go so unchecked and not be monitored by their supervisors and commanders. How could that time be spent viewing pornography when victims were waiting for their cases to be solved? Victims were not having their cases investigated in a timely manner because the investigators assigned to their investigation were more interested in viewing pornography than fulfilling their law enforcement obligation as law enforcement officers.

An internal investigation was conducted, and several investigators were involved in the misconduct. We developed a matrix on the penalty phase of this police conduct. The matrix was mirrored by a similar case in Minnesota, where a department experienced the same sort of police misconduct. The more severe violations would receive days off, and the minor violations would receive letters of reprimand. I believed discipline was an important factor in their abuse of time and misuse of taxpayer dollars. Many individuals approached me during this investigation—public and private—and told me I should terminate every employee. So many individuals told me you would be fired in the private sector if you committed such an act on the company dime.

I looked back at this incident and concluded the officers were not upset over being caught and committing misconduct, but rather why would I stick my nose into their business when they were simply allowed to conduct this behavior without reprisal from their supervisors and commanders? The incident was more about the department's culture and the acceptance that this misconduct was acceptable. It is highly unlikely that the investigators' bosses were unaware that those not even working their assigned case investigations were involved in viewing pornography. If so, the supervisors were sound asleep at the switch or knew about the viewing but ignored it because it was better to go along and get along than rock the boat and do the right thing.

As a side note, the city's Information Technology Department implemented a tracking system after this incident to gauge all city personnel's computer usage. The police department's internet usage took a nose dive, and it was the city's lowest internet user. It's interesting what audit systems can place on behaviors when someone is tracking their activity.

DISCUSSION POINTS

1. Is there an internet protocol in place to view personnel usage?
2. Are sensitive internet access sites alerted to police management?
3. How often do your supervisors conduct work assignments and activities to ensure other non-police-related work is not interfering with actual police work?

MONITORING DRUG INVESTIGATIONS AND INFORMANTS

One of the ways to get your name and agency in the headlines is the inability to manage drug investigators and their informants. There are good law enforcement officers who operate professionally and keep their hands above the table. Unfortunately, a few in our profession do not operate professionally and run afoul of their original oath of office. Although the investigators usually receive the brunt of discipline, the police organization and, specifically, police management are ultimately responsible for police behaviors. Police executives and commanders are responsible for monitoring drug investigations and informants. The lack of managing this important component of an agency will most likely lead to bad outcomes.
Active management of drug investigations should ensure investigators are not assigned to this sensitive position for an extended period of time. You can add or subtract a year on either side, but normally a five-year assignment should be the limit for this sensitive position. Additional time will most likely result in the investigator getting too comfortable and close with informants and the exposure to this complicated type of assigned work.

There is a tendency to become comfortable with informants, especially with opposite-sex individuals. Supervisors should monitor their subordinate investigators and ensure the veracity of their working informants. Investigators should properly register the informant in the department's master informant log. The agency should maintain a policy on working with informants and the parameters. No informant on active parole or probation should be used unless approved by the court. Using an individual on probation or parole could impact the individual's court conditions and place the at-risk person in a potentially compromising position.

One easy method to ensure the integrity of the informant and investigator is to conduct audit checks on the informant's payout form. Ensure the form used to pay the informant is not pre-dated and was completed the same day as the payout. Ensure the form is approved and signed by a supervisor. The supervisor should check the entirety of the form and ensure there is no missing information. If there is missing information, the form should be returned to the investigator, and an immediate response should be provided as to the missing information. A superior commander should then double-check the approved form.

Another safeguard for narcotic investigations is checking and re-checking all items seized in a drug raid/arrest. Every dollar and penny seized from a defendant needs to be placed into evidence. All recovered drugs are to be put into evidence on the day of the recovery. Under no exceptions should unvouchered drugs and money be allowed to be placed into office desk drawers or at any time allow the officer to maintain drugs and money at their residence. All recovered items must be properly identified and placed into the evidence vault immediately after the recovery.

Lastly, all narcotics and money seized during an investigation shall be placed into the department's master evidence and property system.

There is no room or reason for narcotics to maintain a secondary evidence vault, which counters the department's policy and protocol. The department's master evidence and property system ensure proper storage and accountability of seized items. Allowing separate storage outside the master evidence and property system allows for a lack of accountability and what is seized and documented. The same investigator who recovers drugs and money should not be allowed to remove them from their storage area. The master evidence and property system allows for total control, accountability, and the avoidance of someone from removing drugs and money without authorization. All recovered drugs and money can be placed into the department's property system, and if there is ever a need to re-examine the evidence, there is a tracking system to ensure the integrity of the evidence, case arrest, and proper documentation.

DISCUSSION POINTS

1. Does your department have a drug informant policy?
2. Who in the agency is responsible for auditing investigators/ informants?
3. What is the department standard for the length of an assignment in narcotic investigations?
4. Does your agency have an internal audit process to verify informant money is being provided to the individual?
5. Does management review drug informant documents for accuracy and compliance with agency policy?

SUSTAINABILITY

One of the main concerns of a police chief is the sustainability of continual progress toward perfection. You will need to focus on this area to succeed in your overall vision and mission, along with the commitment to constitutional policing. First, you must have strong policies that align with federal, state, and local ordinances. To ensure you have the correct policies, you should consider joining your state accreditation process or Commission Accreditation for Law Enforcement Agencies (CALEA). Both options will ensure you have the personnel, fiscal, operational, community, and other significant professional policing policies within your agency. If you decide to do this on your own, there are model policies available from various law enforcement organizations, which can assist with developing, implementing, and updating agency policies. In any event, survey your current agency policies to ensure your constitutional standards and professional policing models are aligned with the various laws and requirements.

In 2006, I inherited an agency during the process of the initial CALEA accreditation. My predecessor began the initial process, and I thank former Chief Pugh for his willingness to initiate the process for accreditation.

The agency maintained antiquated policies and one that had not been updated since 1972. No agency or police chief should ever allow a policy to elapse from a review beyond one to two years. Laws, regulations, and agencies re-adjust themselves due to community expectations and changes in public policy. It is a disservice to a community for a police chief to maintain policies that have not been reviewed, and carrying policies that have not been updated for over twenty years is unacceptable. Committing to an established review process or associating with an accreditation process will force the issue and the police agency to comply with updated laws, procedures, and practices.

One of the most important areas of sustainability is first-line supervisor oversight. The corporal or sergeant is the first-line supervisor in most agencies and directly impacts the agency's workers (line). The first-line supervisor is directed to carry out the agency's mission, vision, and core issues. The first-line supervisor directs the work of the line and has direct employee connections daily. The first-line supervisor is also most likely in the same bargaining union as the person who directs the workflow. If not, then the first-line supervisor is in a different union than the line officer. In any event, the labor situation raises issues that prevent the first-line supervisor from doing their job effectively. There are many lost opportunities when the first-line supervisor does not coach, mentor, and correct the work activity of their subordinate. You will hear many excuses why a first-line supervisor did not intervene in situations: "I didn't want to tie up radio traffic." "I counseled him on several occasions for the same infraction." "I was too busy to get to that issue." Or "I thought someone else was doing that." As first-line supervisors, we tend to make many excuses instead of just getting the job done. We tend to shy away from controversial issues because that "one" may get me into trouble with my fellow sergeants and officer friends. At the end of their career, many front-line supervisors want and desire the opportunity to flip their steak at the retired police meetings. If you do your job as required, you should not have to worry about the retirement dinners and making sure everyone likes you. As a front-line supervisor, you have a duty to correct the workflow of your subordinates. You have the obligation and responsibility to correct bad behavior in private and praise good behavior in public. You have the duty and responsibility to act and conduct yourself in a manner that protects the welfare of those you supervise. Anything less will likely result in a potential deliberate indifference issue on your part as a supervisor.

A deliberate indifference is an act you commit by not doing something you are responsible for. If you know driving down the wrong way on a one-way street is not allowed by the traffic laws, then you did something you knew was wrong. Because you drove down the one-way street the wrong way, you caused a severe accident with injuries. Now, you are not only wrong for disobeying the law by driving down the wrong way on a one-way street, but you also are responsible for the injury because of your deliberate indifference to your actions. Similarly, as a first-line supervisor, if you fail to recognize and correct the actions of your subordinates, you could be involved in deliberate indifference. For example, as a supervisor, you hear an officer involved in a car pursuit on the radio. The offender is being pursued because the driver threw some garbage out of the window onto the street. The officer attempts to stop the car and cite the driver for littering. The driver avoids the ticket and does not stop for the officer. You hear the reason for the pursuit over the radio and allow the officer to continue. Do you know the current pursuit policy of the agency? Do you know the location of the pursuit? What time of the day is the pursuit taking place? Your inability to inquire about an important issue of the organization could and will potentially impact your police agency.

Establishing long-term sustainability for police agencies involves more than just talk; it involves more than just the chief holding weekly staff meetings and talking about accountability. It's one thing to talk about accountability, but it's another thing to carry out the dynamics of accountability. Accountability starts at the top, and the chief must hold themselves accountable for the process. Whatever you expect your officers to do, you should do similar duties and tasks. If you require your officers to take yearly certification tests, then you, as the chief, should do the same. If you require timelines from your subordinates, then set an example and conduct yourself accordingly. Sustainability starts with the chief and requires the chief to be self-disciplined. And please avoid asking and begging your subordinate commanders to hold individuals accountable. Set the standard on accountability and then let the chips fall.

A police chief must avoid a cozy relationship with the department's special interest groups. Friendliness as a means to stay on the good side of special interest groups is disingenuous and a sign of weak leadership. A chief should stand on their own principles and be their own person, not beholden to the special groups or majority. Sustainability is much different than likability. Sustainability is hard and requires a tremendous amount of courage and tenacity. Likability is easy, requires little effort, and will likely result in a harmonious relationship.

The following provides some opportunities for a police chief to assess and use their sustainability to ensure the police department conducts itself according to twenty-first-century policing standards. At the same time, a community should assess these elements, ensure their police department is performing the following, and then inform the community of the following status:

OUTCOME ASSESSMENTS

MEASUREMENT	COLLECTION & ANALYSIS
USE OF FORCE	• Rate of force used per arrest by the department • Force type by geographic area • Force type by type of arrest, age, sex, and ethnicity • Canine bite ratio • Uses of force that were found to violate department policy and force type • Rate-of-force complaints that are sustained and rates that are not sustained • Number and rate of use-of-force internal investigations in which each finding is supported by a preponderance of the evidence • Number of officers who frequently or repeatedly use force
COMPLAINT PROCESS	• Number and nature of civil litigations against the department and specific officers • Number of judgments or settlements against the city/department • Did any civil litigations result in policy, training, or equipment modifications? • Number of misconduct complaints • Rate of sustained, not sustained, exonerated, and unfounded misconduct complaints • Criminal prosecutions of officers for on- or off-duty conduct
COMMUNITY ENGAGEMENT	• Number and variety of community partnerships • Can the public easily use the department's website to compliment an officer or make a complaint against an officer? • Does the public know the available locations to make a compliment or complaint?
INVESTIGATIONS	• Homicide clearance rate • Domestic violence clearance rate • Number and location of drug search warrants • Number and type of drug arrests by race, gender, and ethnicity
STOPS	• Number of traffic stops. Does the number of reported traffic stops align with state reporting requirements? • Number of pedestrian stops. Does the number of reported pedestrian stops align with state reporting requirements? • Number of police pursuits • Number of police pursuits authorized or denied • Number of pursuits involving an injury to officer/pursued driver/non-involved individual(s)

MEASUREMENT	COLLECTION & ANALYSIS
AUDITING	• Does the agency provide a yearly report/audit for the following: – Master property room – audit all guns, money, and drug; sample size audit of all other seized items in the property room – Bias-based policing – audit of all traffic stops by race, gender, and ethnicity. Location of all stops. Does the number of stops by race proportionally represent the city's population by race? – Use of force – does the agency provide an annual report on

PROBATION AND PAROLE

I gained much appreciation and respect for the probation and parole departments and how they impacted our agency. I immediately learned about the dedicated employees of both agencies who were doing the right thing for the right reasons. I could not understand how the probation and parole process negatively impacted our agency. Our analyst provided valuable data and metrics about those on parole and probation and their impact on criminal incidents. Our mutual working relationship with parole and probation resulted in a better approach to addressing repeat and violent crimes.

There is a difference between probation and parole. Probation, as we know it in state governments, is regulated by a separate unit of government, usually under the control of the county's chief government judge. In Illinois, the chief judge of the court has jurisdictional power and control of the probation department. Individuals are usually placed on probation the first time they commit minor crimes—shoplifting, fighting, and driving under the influence of alcohol. Instead of going to trial, one will plead guilty to their crime and serve time under a set time of probation. A condition of the probation could be alcohol and drug treatment and community service. Primarily, one is placed on probation for a set time, and the individual cannot re-commit their initial crime or any crime while on probation. If someone re-commits a crime and it is minor, normally, the individual will receive a second opportunity and be placed on probation for an extended period of time. During their probation, they are monitored and must report to a probation officer.

On the other hand, if an individual is convicted of a serious crime such as burglary, murder, or shooting someone, they may be sentenced to the department of corrections for prison time. Once released from prison, the individual normally will have a monitoring phase, or parole. A parole officer will monitor their activities, visit their home and ensure they comply with their parole terms. If the individual re-offends during their parole time, they may be placed back into prison and serve their initial full sentence or an extended amount of time in prison.

If the individual is placed on probation or parole, the agency monitoring their activities must know what sort of activity they are involved in during the probation or parole time frame.

We learned quickly that the county probation department maintained a manual system to track and manage those on probation and relied on physical police reports to monitor the activities of those on probation. Our agency had a comprehensive records management system, and we could gather the thousands of names of those on probation and incorporate their information into our records system. In turn, we provided a listing of those on probation back to the department. The probation department was provided a list of names of those probationers who were arrested, a victim, a suspect, and those listed in a police report. The report was generated anytime to the probation department, and they could actively view a current probationer who was involved in a crime, was a suspect in a crime, was a witness to a crime, or was listed in a police report. This was valuable information for the probation department. The probation department could actively view those on probation who were not aligned with the probation requirements. Although we provided a comprehensive list of those on probation involved in a criminal incident, we could not measure the recidivism of those on probation.

If you are on probation and commit an additional crime, the probation department process would normally refer the new crime to the state's attorney's office for review and possible revocation of probation and then charge the individual with the new crime. We were unable to secure the number of referrals brought back to court for a probation revocation. On a daily basis, police officers came across individuals who were on probation for violent crimes. It was important for our department to learn what was occurring with those who re-offended while on probation. Our department tracked the number of arrests and encounters with those on probation and learned the volume of how many encounters of all police events involved those on probation. The department worked well with the probation department and provided them with a vast amount of data to assist those on probation. Future police probation partnerships should build data systems to actively manage those on probation who commit additional offenses while being monitored.

The parole system is similar to the probation process but with a few differences. First, we found those on parole may have committed their initial crime in another county but were paroled to our county. I could not understand why there was an influx of "out of jurisdiction" offenders coming to our county for their parole. I remember asking this question to a prison official near our city and was told that they were attracted to the outreach services available in our county. Because of the outreach services, an individual could come to a county on parole and live and work while on parole.

DISCUSSION POINTS

1. Does your local probation department maintain a robust records management system that can tie into your police department's system?

2. Of those on probation, how many re-offend yearly, and of those who re-offend, how many are referred to the court for probation revocation?

POLICE APPLICANT BACKGROUND CHECKS

Police chiefs leading law enforcement agencies have enormous pressures, responsibilities, and duties. One of the most important decisions they will make is hiring sworn and non-sworn personnel. Unfortunately, many police officers have resigned and retired because of the current climate with police-community relations. Additionally, some police officers have quit the profession because they cannot withstand the scrutiny of police reforms in order to make the policing industry better for all. Although police agencies have struggled to maintain adequate staffing levels, the mass exodus of personnel might be a positive aspect of our industry. We should not expect or approve of less than constitutional and professional policing for our communities. Those officers who either cannot support police reforms or cannot withstand the constant scrutiny should and have left the force. This is good for our policing industry and the betterment of effective relations with our communities. To ensure we hire the best and forget about the rest, police departments must ensure a complete and comprehensive applicant background examination.

Conducting police applicant background checks is one of the most overlooked risk management issues from a chief law enforcement executive's perspective. A police applicant background check is one of the most important decisions made by the chief executive. I have often heard from police chiefs that it is too expensive to conduct out-of-state background checks on a potential applicant. Sending someone out of state to check on an applicant does not fit into the annual budget. This response and attitude are wrong and apathetic and could result in the agency paying more in the long run than the initial background check expense. One of the most important decisions of a law enforcement executive is determined by the decision of who you hire. Further, who you hire will impact the future of the agency either positively or negatively. The same is true for the hiring of non-sworn personnel. Non-sworn applicants should receive the same background process as sworn applicants.

Who you hire now will most likely cause future issues. For example, a potential police applicant applied to a department, was successful in the hiring process, and would be provided employment pending a background investigation. The background investigator traveled out of state to conduct the investigation, which was a wise decision by the agency at the time. The unwise and ridiculous decision was to hire the applicant regardless of the background investigation's findings. The investigator conducted a thorough interview and noted disconcerting actions by the applicant. Unfortunately, we employed the applicant even though the background investigation revealed the applicant as having high-risk issues, which eventually became evident in our eventual hire.

DISCUSSION POINTS

1. Provide a comprehensive background investigation on all police applicants, regardless of their applying geographic location.
2. Consider contracting with other law enforcement agencies to conduct the background check if the geographic distance is far from your agency.

RISK MANAGEMENT

Communicating and having supervisors understand the importance of risk management was a difficult challenge. The term was foreign to some personnel, and they lacked the understanding of supervising and holding subordinates responsible for their actions. Missed opportunities by supervisors cost the city millions of dollars in actual and associated costs in risk management because of not supervising correctly. There was a strong culture of not looking back, especially without critically analyzing oneself. There was much hesitation in critiquing personnel's actions, referred to as "Monday night quarterbacking." Interestingly, when a SWAT team rollout was completed, the team would reassemble and critique what took place. I often mentioned to our supervisors/command staff that if critiquing was good for a SWAT rollout, then why couldn't we apply that same approach to everyday police operations? There were a few in the organization who got it, but it was a small group of professionals who did a good job by ensuring the actions of others were done professionally. Unfortunately, some in positions of authority didn't get it, which cost the city not only in lost dollars but also doing the right thing at the right time. Those same individuals worried more about themselves than their oath of office and the citizens they served.

I have provided a checklist below to assist you as a current or aspiring police chief. At the same time, the checklist will provide community residents with a way to gauge their police agency.

CRITICAL RISK ISSUES

CRITICAL RISK COMPONENT	ASSESSMENT	SUGGESTED PRACTICE
POLICE APPLICANT BACKGROUND INVESTIGATIONS	Over the years, I have been amazed at the police agencies who do not conduct thorough and complete police applicant background investigations. Further, many police agencies do not conduct out-of-state background investigations on applicants due to financial decisions.	• Conduct a background investigation on every police applicant. • |Do not consider the distance from your agency to where the applicant is applying; conduct an on-site background investigation. • Assess current and former neighbors, associates, employers, etc. • Document all conversations
COMPLAINT PROCESS	Does your agency have an open complaint system where residents can file a complaint/commendation online, in person, or from strategic locations in your community? Does your community know how to file a complaint? Has the police department engaged the community in this?	• Establish online complaint and compliment reporting. • Provide reporting portals throughout your community. • Provide documents in varied languages of your community.
USE OF FORCE	Does your agency track all uses of force beyond normal handcuffing? Does your agency respond to intermediate and serious uses of force with a supervisory investigation? Does your agency provide use-of-force reviews for serious uses of force from the perspective of training, tactics, and policy?	• Establish a use-of-force policy. • Establish yearly training. • Maintain current training lesson plans. • Report all uses of force beyond compliant handcuffing. • Ensure supervisors are trained in investigating a use-of-force incident. • Train supervisors/commanders on how to evaluate and critique a use-of-force incident for reviews.
INSPECTIONS AND REVIEWS	Don't expect what you don't inspect. Does your agency make periodic inspections and reviews of use-of-force incidents, police stops, drug informants, undercover drug operations, crime statistics, sexual assault investigations, random calls for service, and internal investigations?	• Property and evidence audits. • Police informant audits. • Stop, search, and arrest audits. • Crime reporting audits. • Case closure audits.

CRITICAL RISK COMPONENT	ASSESSMENT	SUGGESTED PRACTICE
POLICIES	Does your agency have policies to cover the essentials of a police department? Does your agency have policies on use of force, procedural justice, evidence handling, criminal investigations, police pursuits, complaint investigations, juvenile procedures, and civic engagement?	• Ensure policies can withstand public scrutiny. • Ensure you have a policy covering your agency's administrative, personnel, operational, tactical, and training components. • Ensure policies are reviewed yearly.
PROBLEM-SOLVING	Problem-solving is one of the most overlooked aspects of policing. If you do not attack a problem strategically, the problem will linger and become much more complex.	• Ensure your agency incorporates the functions of SARA: scan, analyze, respond, assess. • Monthly public meetings should be convened to discuss ongoing quality of life issues, traffic concerns, repeat calls, and overall violent and property crime assessments.
SUPERVISION	How do you prepare future leaders in your agency? What types of pre-training do you provide for those who wish to lead?	• Provide a least a 120-hour in-service training session for new first-line supervisors. The training should include human relations, management, Internal Affairs, operations, coaching, and mentoring aspects of current industry trends, agency practice, policy, and protocols. The sessions should include adult-learning principles and opportunities to practice and role-play. • Middle-management promotions should include refresher training on all mentioned areas and provide discussions for growth opportunities for personnel.
WELLNESS	Productive employees are influenced and impacted by their personal and professional lifestyles. The pressures of law enforcement are enormous, and agencies should provide opportunities for stress relief, health, and wellness focus for employees.	• Agencies should consider periodic sessions to employees on nutrition, medical, and exercise wellness. Emphasizing good nutritious food will assist in the wellness of personnel.

CRITICAL RISK COMPONENT	ASSESSMENT	SUGGESTED PRACTICE
COMMUNITY ENGAGEMENT	Do you know who your chief of police is? When did you last see the chief on social media discussing crime concerns? How accessible is the chief of police? Can you pick up the phone and speak to who is in command of your residential/business area? How do you report ongoing crime issues, and how are the results provided to you?	• Every department should have a strategic plan on how they will engage with their community. • Community surveys should be taken to gauge the community's connection with the police department. • How does the community interact with the police department and relay their requests to the department? • How is this information publicly transmitted for all to know?
TRAINING	Training is an important component of law enforcement. Training is an ongoing cycle that ensures personnel are aware of current laws, procedures, protocols, and systems to carry out their law enforcement duties effectively.	• A department should maintain the following training: – Level-entry post academy – Field training officer – Initial investigator – First-line supervisor – Mid-level supervisor – Yearly criminal, tactical, operational, and department protocol – Annual use-of-force, bias-based policing, procedural justice, critical incident, mentally ill, criminal law, and human relations

Challenge yourself as a current police chief. Challenge yourself as an aspiring police chief. Challenge yourself as a resident of your community to hold the police accountable for their actions.

I really enjoy the quote from the late Robert Kennedy: "Every society gets the kind of criminal it deserves. What is equally true is that every community gets the kind of law enforcement it insists on."

REFERENCES LIST

1. "Program Profile: Rockford (Ill.) Area Violence Elimination Network (RAVEN), National Institute of Justice, August 29, 2022, https://crimesolutions.ojp.gov/ratedprograms/766#eo.

2. Ritter, Nancy. "CeaseFire: A Public Health Approach to Reduce Shootings and Killings," *National Institute of Justice Journal*, October 28, 2009, https://nij.ojp.gov/topics/articles/ceasefire-public-health-approach-reduce-shootings-and-killings.

3. Rockford Police Pursuit Policy, 2015.

4. Sweeney, Chuck. "Chuck Sweeny: Report gives 27 ways to build better cop shop," *Rockford Register Star*, June 17, 2010, https://www.rrstar.com/story/opinion/columns/guest/2010/06/17/chuck-sweeny-report-gives-27/42658280007/.

ACKNOWLEDGMENTS

This book could not have been completed without the following individuals: Mayor Lawrence J. Morrissey and his entire team for their support, loyalty, and willingness to tackle the big issues of accountability, police reform, and providing excellence everywhere for everyone; Attorney Jonathan S. Aronie, Attorney David L. Douglass, Chief Dennis Nowicki and Chief Charles A. Gruber for allowing me to provide expertise, knowledge and experience in police consent decree matters. Dr. Alexander Weiss for his wisdom and common-sense approach to police organizational design, development, and strategy, Professor Robert Evans for his years of public policy discussions; Lieutenant Daniel T. Gray for his friendship and challenging thought-process. Chief McCullum for his encouragement and support during my time as chief and now as a litigation consultant; Attorney John Coyne for my first litigation trial and keen wisdom and approach in the legal arena; Police Information Management Administrator Roger Ratze his for deep knowledge on data science and his steadfast support in the completion of the book; Lloyd Johnson for his professional friendship and allowance to build a strong bond between the NAACP and the police department; Reverend K. Edward Copeland for his tremendous support for fair and equitable policing for all; Poor Clare Colettine Nuns of Rockford for their many prayers.

ABOUT THE AUTHOR

Chief Chet Epperson (Ret.)

Chief Epperson is an experienced 42-year police professional in areas of use of force, internal affairs, officer-involved shootings, supervision, wrongful convictions, practice, policy, discipline, mental health, auditing, staffing analysis, organizational assessments, investigations, and training. Chief Epperson began his police career in 1981 as a police cadet with the Rockford, Illinois Police Department. Due to the city financial and personnel hiring freeze, Chief Epperson was hired as a patrol officer with the Lake Forest, Illinois Police Department. Chief Epperson was then re-hired in 1985 by the Rockford Police Department as a patrol officer. Chief Epperson served as a field training officer and trained over twenty-five new officers until he as promoted to sergeant, lieutenant, deputy chief, and in 2006 appointed as chief of police. Chief Epperson was instrumental in the department receiving initial law enforcement accreditation and subsequent renewals for continued compliance with law enforcement standards. He was instrumental in internal police reforms to include an early warning system, community policing initiatives, problem solving, and a robust use-of-force process including supervisory investigations, administrative reviews, and use-of-force review board. Chief Epperson retired in 2015.

Chief Epperson is the President, Americans for Effective Law Enforcement (AELE). Formed in 1966, AELE is a research-driven educational organization that produces and disseminates legal information through traditional seminars, via electronic media and direct contact. On-going experience for the past 7-years as a police practice consultant providing Federal District Court-Appointed monitoring expertise in police consent decrees and a United States Department of Justice Civil Rights police consultant regarding police use of force. Expert in applying constitutional standards, state law, policy, practice and training to police incidents. Retained in plaintiff and defense litigation occurrences. Chief Epperson regularly instructs courses on police use of force, internal affairs, discipline, and risk-management issues. Chief Epperson performs police management assessments on staffing, operations, policy, auditing, investigations, and training.

Printed in the United States
by Baker & Taylor Publisher Services